TESTIMONIALS

I had the pleasure and privilege of meeting Pastor Ajai Prakash and his wife, Maureena, and interviewing him about his ministry near North Liberty, Iowa, and of their efforts to bring the Word of God to willing ears in the Middle East. The dangers they faced, from traversing unforgiving terrai, to threats from an anti-Christian ideology, had me riveted.

While I've met and interviewed many ministers and pastors in my work as a small-town newspaper reporter, the depth of faith of this remarkable couple has been unequaled. Their story is not one of "here's what we did" for the glorification of themselves. Far from it. Their story is one of struggle, of sacrifice, of willingly going into the bear cage knowing full well they may not make it back out. Their story glorifies God and the spirit of men and women willing to not only partake of it, but fight for it.

It is not only a journal of times and places in their past, but also have a prophetic note; intentional or not, which speaks to the present day. With Islam seemingly on the rise in America, and daily attacks against Christianity becoming the norm, Pastor Prakash seems to be sounding a warning. Could a land of "underground churches" become reality here? Are people willing to risk everything, to give up everything, for the sake of living and proclaiming God's Word?

This is a story worth reading, and it not only chronicles one couples' journey of faith, it may launch one of your own as well.

—Christopher D. Umscheid
Reporter-Photographer, Solon Economist,
North Liberty Leader Newspapers,
Clarence, IA

When a person buys a piece of land, puts a big beautiful house on it, and moves in, they are settled in to stay. They would do anything to protect what they own, their investment. Pastor Ajai Prakash is like that person. He has invested time, emotions, will, money, and his life in the kingdom of God! Pastor Ajai loves Jesus with all his heart and stands on the Word of God. Pastor Ajai preaches and teaches pure gospel. Because of the path the Lord has placed him on, you can be assured that he is a man after God's own heart. I would recommend that you invest some time in reading his book and you will be blessed, impressed, and strengthen in your own walk with Christ.

—J. D. Warling
Station manager of KSKB, 99.1,
Christian radio, Brooklyn, IA

Surrender all, suffer, and serve the Father God as our Lord and Savior Jesus Christ who will transform our hearts to cross over to His security and sobriety. Pastor Ajai and Maureena's story in this book shows a living example of truly being a disciple of Jesus Christ. Your soul will be ignited and energized and you will get to know Jesus Christ and the Holy Spirit in a personal way.

—Dr. Darrell Winterowd
DVM; shares love through animals and the
local television media, Cedar Rapids, IA

I would encourage reading Ajai and Maureena's story and find out how God led them through adversity and hardship and honed their faith as hardened steel is forged. This is a riveting true adventure that is not yet finished.

—Frank Stephen
Law enforcement, businessman,
and missionary with OM, Swisher, IA

A helpful tool to understand the Islamic faith in comparison to Christianity and become more effective in ministering to Muslims in the USA and overseas.

—Edwin A Humpleby
Realtor with Ruhl & Ruhl Realtors,
Coralville, IA

THE UNDERGROUND TENTMAKERS

THE
UNDERGROUND
TENTMAKERS

A Missionary Journey From
The Middle East To The Midwest

AJAI PRAKASH

TATE PUBLISHING
AND ENTERPRISES, LLC

Published by Tate Publishing & Enterprises, LLC
127 E. Trade Center Terrace | Mustang, Oklahoma 73064 USA
1.888.361.9473 | www.tatepublishing.com

Tate Publishing is committed to excellence in the publishing industry. The company reflects the philosophy established by the founders, based on Psalm 68:11,
"The Lord gave the word and great was the company of those who published it."

Book design copyright © 2013 by Tate Publishing, LLC. All rights reserved.
Cover design by Rtor Maghuyop
Interior design by Caypeeline Casas

Published in the United States of America

ISBN: 978-1-62746-998-2
1. category:sub category
2. category: sub category
13.07.09

DEDICATION

To all those who risk their lives for Christ in hostile nations and continue to put their lives on the line even today...

> For I am not ashamed of the gospel of Christ, for it is the power of God to salvation for everyone who believes, for the Jew first and also for the Greek.
>
> Romans 1:16

> Be faithful until death, and I will give you the crown of life.
>
> Revelation 2:10

ACKNOWLEDGMENTS

"Can two walk together, unless they are agreed?"

Amos 3:3

Just where do we start to thank those that joined us, walked beside us, and assisted us along the way? Here I pen down decades of thoughts of those that I have been a laborer and servant of the Lord with, and share my insights into the underground ministry in the Middle East. So at last, here it is.

Perhaps the pages in this book will be seen as an appreciation to those of you who have facilitated in soul winning, transformational conversions, and making Christ's tentmaking ministry what is today.

I cannot thank my wife, Maureena, enough, one who has covenanted to walk with me till death do us part, a partner in crime who continually stands by me even when I stand alone. She is a pillar of strength and support, an inspiring force from the start of the book, and whose gentle critique has brought forth the best.

A big thank you to our mentors, Brother Ebenezer Vijay and Ambu, for their invaluable support. They taught us to develop a lifestyle of prayer, walk the narrow path, be passionate for God, and love Him with all our heart, might, soul, and strength.

I take immense pleasure in thanking Sunny Singh, my nephew, worship leader, and partner in ministry to encourage, analyze, and throw light on contemporary editing and book publishing in the 21st century.

Apart from my own efforts, I am sincerely grateful to Ryan Adair for dedicatedly editing, critiquing, and setting the narrative in motion. And my gratitude goes out to Mitch Moylan for summarizing, critiquing the language, flow, and content of the manuscript.

I wish to express my sincere gratitude to my preaching team: Glenn Pettit, Rob Hansen, and Mitch Moylan for taking the effort in bracing themselves to preach on Sundays when I had taken time off to write this book.

I wish to personally thank Chris Umscheid for inspiration, motivation, and his tone of genuine urgency for me to finish writing.

I am immensely grateful to the leadership team of my church—Karen and Troy Langos, Jack Lekin, Frank Stephen, Brother Edwin Humpleby, Glenn Pettit, and Kyle Bantz—in remaining faithful and persevering during hard times. They have whole-heartedly encouraged and supported the vision of this book and filled in by taking on more ministerial responsibilities.

My humble appreciation goes out to Dr. Samuel Schutz and Dr. Aida Spencer for their encouraging directions, advice, and helpful critique.

I am indebted to the body of Christ at The Well, in Swisher, Iowa, for giving me ample time and support through their prayers and encouragement during the writing of this manuscript.

Finally, a word of gratitude goes forth to our parents, our families, and friends for their understanding and support to us while completing this book. Without their help, I would face many difficulties in effectively accomplishing this manuscript.

CONTENTS

FOREWORD

by Timothy C. Tennant, PhD

I first met Pastor Ajai Prakash as a student when I was a professor at Gordon-Conwell Theological Seminary. I instantly recognized his deep passion for the Lord as well as his remarkable story. It is truly astounding that a young man would go to the Gulf to work and find Jesus Christ in one of the least Christian countries in the world.

This book is the story of his journey. However, you should not read this amazing account as you would a normal biography. It is not really a story about Ajai and Maureena Prakash, as it is about the marvelous providence of God. This is an account which beautifully demonstrates how the mission of God in the world intersects with our own personal histories in profound and moving ways. This account will encourage you to see the hand of God at work in your own life and to trust Him in deeper ways.

—Timothy C. Tennent, PhD
President, Asbury Theological Seminary
Wilmore, Kentucky

FOREWORD

by Dr. Samuel R. Schutz

Pastor Ajai Prakash has written a fascinating and creative novel, and what makes it most exciting is that the novel is actual history rather than mere fiction. This is his own story, an autobiographical account of extraordinary love, passion, adventure, and, above all, God's powerful blessing upon his life.

Pastor Ajai's greatest passion is for his Lord, the God of Abraham and Isaac and Jacob, the God of all nations from the north and the south and the east and the west, and the God of his own beloved nation of India. This is the story of God's calling Pastor Ajai out of darkness and into life as he committed himself completely to the Triune God through saving faith in our Lord Jesus Christ. This is the story of God's calling him into gospel ministry and extraordinary opportunity to bring the saving gospel of Christ to nations normally closed to Christian mission. This is the story of how God has sent him and his wife, Maureena, from India to become missionaries to us in the USA.

Pastor Ajai's life has been made all the more extraordinary through the earthly love of his life, his precious and equally gifted wife, Maureena. I have had the opportunity to know them both and to claim them as Christian brother and sister and close friends. Pastor Ajai and Maureena's love for one another is exemplary for the entire church to whom God sends them. Together, they hear from God through His Word in the Holy Scriptures, they hear from God through the ministry of the Holy Spirit, and they follow the Lord unequivocally and without reservation as He directs their steps. No sacrifice is too great for them to make, and with every sacrifice comes greater joy for them to share with others. Their ministry is so effective because of the authenticity of their daily lives so that they can say with the apostle Paul, "Imitate me, just as I also imitate Christ" (1 Corinthians 11:1).

I pray that this book will be used by our Lord to inspire and challenge God's people far and wide to follow Christ uncompromisingly, and to sacrifice all for Him for God's glory. Loving redemptive sacrifice with joy is God's chosen means, through His church, for His kingdom to come and His will to be done on earth as it is in heaven. Glory to our Lord with all honor and praise!

—Dr. Samuel R. Schutz
Professor of Evangelism and Church Planting
Gordon-Conwell Theological Seminary
South Hamilton, Massachusetts

THE ARISING UNDERGROUND CHURCH

The church we know in the West is very much unlike the church throughout the rest of the world. We enjoy the pleasures of freedom and all the trappings that come along with it. For the most part, our investment is what brings comfort to the majority and allows them to feel good about themselves. A simple definition of this is called "humanism."

Humanism is defined as "a philosophy that usually rejects supernaturalism and stresses an individual's dignity, worth, and capacity for self-realization through reason." In other words, it's completely self-focused and self-absorbed. It has very little to do with suffering and even less with self-examination and conviction of what is truly detrimental based on absolute truths from God's Word.

But at the same time, a humanistic gospel has emerged in the West while the true gospel is still alive and active throughout the world. It has not been lost or tainted, nor has it been twisted to bring a certain crowd with itching ears. No, it has endured through persecution, suffering, and hardship. This book is just about that—the story of enduring truth and how that truth was protected at all costs.

God has a plan that is unfolding within the earth. It is strategic and all-inclusive. It is dynamic and full of life. It holds the answers that are needed in this moment and brings a relevant message. The question is this: Will it be accepted because it is coming from an unexpected place? It is being placed in the hearts of a faithful few who are willing to pay any price, go anywhere, and do anything. Unlike most who demand certain returns, these are unselfish carriers of truth.

As God has reached toward many to be vessels of change, He now is reaching to a group of people to be carriers of the final move of God upon the earth. These carriers are rising as a remnant from within the United States, but many are coming from other nations as well. There is a remnant of uncompromising believers, much like the seven thousand that did not bow their knee to Baal. They have not lost hope or watered down their message, but maintain the standard of holiness required in this hour. They have a clear picture of the need and also the answer for this hour. Like the sons of Issachar, they have been positioned upon the earth in this moment to understand the times and seasons, knowing what must be done (1 Chronicles 12:32).

This unappreciated group sees themselves as missionaries to those in need of God, yet denies or is unaware of their need. They have maintained purity of truth and uncompromising faith in other nations, where what they believe may cause their life to be taken from them. The territory they see themselves called to is unexpected, yet in great need—the United States of America.

This group of ministers is coming into our midst from other nations. They are seeing a great mission field before them, an untapped arena of opportunity that is not being touched. There are multitudes in the valley of decision, waiting on a messenger from God to bring them hope. But they also see a second mission field, and that is the church itself, a church that is in need of reform and to be awakened. They see a church that at one time was the agent of change for the nations, but is now a mission field itself. Those we have sown into for years are now returning to us to save us from ourselves before it is too late.

In this hour, there is an emerging underground church that few realize is forming. It is a church that has an uncompromising message and approach due to the hardships they have endured for their faith. Unlike the typical Western church that has compromised most of what it believes for money, prestige, or numerical growth, this church has an agenda that is focused upon the kingdom and intentions of God upon the earth.

This book is that story—the story of enduring love toward their Savior. It is a story of the church—what it really looks like and what it is to accomplish. This story is a story of hope for change and the plan of God still unfolding upon the earth. As you read these pages, may it not be mere words to inform you; but may you realize there are actual lives that, by experience, suffering, and endurance, have created the words and the stories.

May your heart be gripped and may you allow yourself to be examined by the Holy Spirit's convicting power!

—Greg Crawford, Ph.D.
Author of 11 books and
Founder of Jubilee International Ministries,
Jubilee School of Ministry, and
Jubilee International School of Ministry
Overseer of The Base, Des Moines, IA

CHAPTER 1

JUST MARRIED

There are three things which are too wonderful
for me, yes, four which I do not understand: the
way of an eagle in the air, the way of a serpent
on a rock, the way of a ship in the midst of the
sea, and the way of a man with a virgin.

Proverbs 30:18–19

He who finds a wife finds a good thing, and
obtains favor from the Lord.

Proverbs 18:22

Weddings in India are monumental events. Perhaps
this is because marriage in Indian culture happens only
once in a lifetime. There is a lot of preparation leading
up to the wedding day. After I had finished graduate
studies and Maureena was in her final year of nursing,
we were formally engaged in the summer of 1986. We
had waited with prayer and anticipation for seven years
of courtship before getting married on Wednesday,
May 10, 1989.

We planned a very simple wedding. It was a hot and
sultry day, but nothing could change our joy that this
day had finally arrived. Calvary Church on Brown Road[1]

was brimming with people from all faiths and cultural backgrounds, waiting for our wedding to take place. Many of those in the sanctuary had never attended a formal Christian wedding. We were thrilled that they would get to see this God-ordained institution being officially played out in our lives as we said our marriage vows, pledging our love before God and man.

My immediate family, relatives, friends, the best man, and I all walked into the church at 5 o'clock sharp. I was wearing a grey suit with a crimson red necktie; the best man was dressed in off-white. The wedding was scheduled for 5:30 p.m.

The bridal entourage walked into the sanctuary at 5:30 p.m. on the dot, and the march began as the pipe organs played at full volume. Maureena was wearing a milky white sari and a lovely veil. Her brother Justin escorted her to the altar. Three pastors confirmed and endorsed our wedding that day—Pastor Noel, Pastor Abraham, and Pastor Stephen, who officiated the wedding. There was a lot of Scripture reading that took place, and the pastors expounded on the role of the husband and wife in a Christian marriage. The hour and a half ceremony seemed to fly by.

After we vowed "till death do us part," Maureena and I went for a ride and returned 30 minutes later. She changed her clothes and put on a bright red sari— she looked stunning in both dresses she wore that day. After the ceremony, we continued with the wedding banquet, cake-cutting, receiving of gifts, and mingling with family and friends.

The wedding was now over. The sun had set and it was getting dark. But the most difficult part was yet to come—Maureena would leave her family and go with me. The hour of separation is always emotional for the family. After the wedding banquet, both of our immediate families proceeded to Maureena's parental home, which was near the banquet hall. We had a short time of prayer and the final greeting of family before we left. Maureena's mother and sisters wept as though they were never going to see her again, but Maureena had an unbelievable composure.

As we drove away, I asked her, "Maureena, why didn't you get emotional with all that was going on with your family?"

Her answer didn't surprise me. "Oh," she said, "I had to wait seven long years for this day. Finally, I am your wife. I am going to be with you as long as I live. I am so happy that nothing could make me upset or sad today!"

I knew her heart was overflowing with joy just as mine was. We were both eager to begin our life together. We briefly stopped at my parents' home to thank them for all their help with the wedding and to say goodbye before heading off to our hotel. Being completely exhausted, we needed respite for the next few days.

Our marriage wasn't a fairy tale by any means. Married life was not easy for either of us; it was complicated. We were two individuals coming together to live as a married couple under one roof. We brought with us the baggage of our familial upbringings, cultures, and distinct backgrounds. We were different in so many ways, but our common ground was our intense and passionate faith in Jesus Christ. Our love for one another rested on this alone. We agreed on our spiritual understanding of Christ and His Word—our marriage depended on it.

The first month of married life was the toughest. We had some unresolved family issues that strained our relationship. Both of us recognized this, but we were reluctant to make the needed changes. I was intense, quick-tempered, and just plain hardheaded. Maureena was calm but often overreacted when things didn't go her way. It was so easy to unleash our raw emotions on each other. We finally came to a consensus that what we needed was time in prayer, meditating on God's Word, and seeking His guidance in all these surfacing family issues.

We not only had to pray, but we had to work on eliminating the ungodly works of the flesh, striving to manifest the fruit of the Holy Spirit. One of the most important aspects we had to focus on was genuinely surrendering every area of our lives to Christ. This entailed a prodigious effort on our part to make the right choices. It wasn't easy or straightforward; this transformation could take weeks, months, or even years.

We set our minds to it, however, determined that with God's help we would overcome this hurdle. We gave each other sufficient time alone for reflection, self-examination, and prayer. Our goal was to have the mind of Christ in order to work out our differences— to have the issues straightened out in our minds and our hearts right with God. We had to be patient with one another, practice humility, and work on unlearning negative emotions.

Unfortunately, we had no mentors or elderly guidance through this time. Due to the absence of premarital, marital, or family counseling, we were trying to figure out married life all on our own. We knew we needed divine guidance, godly intervention, and to apply His Word. And what we learned was how awesome God is when we come to the throne of grace, earnestly seeking to do His will. We asked and He answered. He was faithful through it all.

We traveled about 180 miles to Mussoorie[2] for our marriage celebrations at the end of June. My youngest sister and grandfather accompanied us, and we stayed with my sister Noor. Needless to say, things didn't go as planned. One afternoon, contentions developed among the siblings about some family issues, making our stay extremely uncomfortable. Because of this, we decided to leave and return back home.

During the journey back, our bus broke down, causing us to reach Ambala too late to catch the last bus home. We were able to obtain some information and immediately tried to board the next train home. One of the trains going home was about to arrive on the railway platform, but it didn't matter because the ticket-checker asked us for a bribe to land a seat.

By this time, Maureena was running a high fever and we didn't know what to do. So we waited for an empty passenger train to arrive. We traveled the entire night, meandering through all the villages of Punjab before we arrived at Ludhiana the following morning. After we reached home, we got medical help for Maureena. This was one of the worst trips we had ever made.

Now that we were done with summer vacation, Maureena and I were ready to move ahead in life. Maureena rejoined her work of teaching potential nurses at the College of Nursing at the Christian Medical College, and I resumed teaching at Sacred Heart for Boys. We settled back into our small studio apartment we had immediately moved into after getting married.[3]

Every day we went to sleep early and got up before daybreak. I drove Maureena to one end of the city on a handed down, broken apart moped, and then rode across the city to where I worked. The everyday ordeal became exhausting and wore us out. We had no other alternative but to stick where we were and continue to do what we were doing.

During this period of our life, we experienced difficult days. Sometimes we didn't have enough money to buy whole milk, eggs, or meat. We consumed cheap, skimmed milk, ate lentils and veggies, and did not have enough money to buy a fridge or a water cooler. Our only financial support came from our petty-paying jobs. We had no choice but to work hard and rely on God alone, who we knew would do the impossible in our lives in His perfect time.

Months flew by before we thought of buying a scooter, but nobody was ready to be the underwriter for procuring a loan from the bank. Having begged friends and family to stand as our guarantor, no one trusted a young couple like us. Such circumstances discouraged us. Finally, after a lot of prayer, we approached one of my coworkers, whose cousin was a bank manager, and he helped get us the loan to purchase a new scooter. It became our lifeline to and from work. God was faithful to us once again.

Soon thereafter, our married life began picking up momentum. We spent six days of the week at our jobs and one day attending church and doing all the weekly chores. In reality, we didn't have a single day of genuine rest and recuperation before going back to work. We worked hard with little salary and no return, living hand-to-mouth, but we were happy together. In our busy schedule, we also had to steal time to meet our parents and siblings. Despite all of this, time flew by and life moved even faster.

I tutored English and social studies students during the evenings to make extra money just to make ends meet. It helped cover the rise in the cost of living, helping us move forward. But still, there was no profound blessing in the extra money.

We began to think of having a better life—this kind of lifestyle was not conducive for us to have children, as we desired to give them the best. We knew that if we continued like this, we would not be able to afford a home or make any investments for retirement. Maureena and I also prayed and thought that one or both of us would have to go overseas to make money in order to fulfill our dream of having our own home and becoming a financially sound family.[4]

One evening, during the spring of 1990, as my father returned from work, he stopped at our studio apartment to give us a tiny newspaper clipping of some interviews being conducted in Delhi for nurses who intended to go to the Middle East.[5] We were interested but didn't really know how to pursue it as Maureena was running a fever and the interviews were being held the following morning almost 200 miles away in New Delhi. We went to my parental home to further discuss the matter, but due to Maureena's fever I was reluctant to travel to Delhi that night.

After a lot conversation, however, Maureena and I left that night. We traveled without any prior reservations and didn't get any rest at all. The next morning we arrived in New Delhi and proceeded to our destination. Maureena, with all the necessary paperwork, went to the interview hall. Everything went so well.

The interview board informed her that she would get a call to go to Bombay for a written exam and have even more interviews. After her preliminary interview in Delhi, we breathed a sigh of relief, had a quick bite at a local dhaba,[6] and met my aunt and uncle before returning home. After traveling over eight hours, we arrived back home and were hopeful to see better days ahead.

We waited patiently for many months to hear from the Delhi office for overseas employment, but nothing arrived. I had even written to the director without any response. On one of my trips to Delhi, I made it a point to visit their office and see what was really going on. After meeting with the director, I learned that things were moving slowly at the government office in the

Middle East. They needed to get legal approval for employing foreign nurses in their hospitals.

Late one summer day, we received a letter for Maureena to go to Bombay for further examinations. We were excited, but immediately learned that I could not accompany her on this trip because I had my final exams during that same time. It was decided that my father would escort her to Bombay, and they would stay at my uncle and aunt's place in Borivili. Maureena passed with flying colors and waited for orders to fly to the Middle East, which could happen any day.

In the meantime, I learned that I did exceptionally well on my education exams and consequently obtained a graduate degree in education. I sensed a great accomplishment in establishing myself in this field. The Catholic school I worked for promoted me to be the supervisor of the middle school there. It was fun, but a greater responsibility was shifted onto my shoulders. I thought I had finally started to climb the academic corporate ladder.

Things were beginning to move in the direction we had been longing for. We didn't really know where all this would take us, but one thing was sure: we had finally started to move on the professional conveyor belt.

We often felt incapable and humbled, but knew that God had His hand upon our lives and He would never leave us or forsake us. Time flew by at work and our day-to-day activities; but whenever we thought about Maureena moving to the Middle East, nothing seemed to be happening. The days turned into weeks, and the weeks turned into months. The waiting held us on the edge of our seat. But it finally paid off in the fall of the same year. Maureeena received an appointment letter in the mail to join the nursing staff of a hospital in a country of the Arabian Peninsula.

Many thoughts raced through our minds. We wondered whether we were being impatient with our lives or whether such a decision was even the right thing to do. The thought of Maureena living alone in some unknown place in the Middle East was scary, not to mention it made me uneasy. Hearing stories of young women going to the Middle East for jobs and their bodies returning back in coffins under mysterious circumstances made me concerned for her security there.

Both of us also had feelings of apprehension as we approached the time where we would be separated for months, or possibly even years, in the coming future. Some of these feelings were counteracted by the possibility of having our own home and a better lifestyle. We even thought about how moving in this direction would provide bright prospects for our kids in the future.

A lot of thoughts flooded our minds—we had to make a choice. At this point, the most vital question of our life was: Will these audacious steps of faith make our life, or destroy it? Godly discernment was the key we needed.

CHAPTER 2

RELOCATION DURING WAR

A time to love, and a time to hate; a time of war, and a time of peace.

Ecclesiastes 3:8

Better is a little with the fear of the Lord, than great treasure with trouble.

Proverbs 15:16

For where your treasure is, there your heart will be also.

Matthew 6:21

On August 2, 1990, under the cover of darkness, Iraq invaded Kuwait. Something the world had not anticipated just begun. Most people around the world were in shock, waiting with anticipation as to what would happen next. People looked upon America and waited to see their response to this Iraqi aggression. It was clear as to why this incursion had transpired.

By the time the ceasefire with Iran was signed in August 1988, Iraq was virtually bankrupt, with most of its debt owed to Saudi Arabia and Kuwait. Iraq pressured both nations to forgive the debts, but they refused. They also accused Kuwait of exceeding its OPEC quotas and driving down the price of oil, thus having a catastrophic impact on the Iraqi economy. The Iraqi government described it as a form of economic warfare, which it claimed was aggravated by Kuwait slant drilling across the border into Iraq's Rumaila oil field.[7]

Iraqis were also allegedly eyeballing Saudi Arabia. Intimidation was rising and there was always a possibility of an assault on the Saudis. On August 31, negotiations between Iraq and Kuwait in Jeddah, Saudi Arabia, failed violently. The upcoming all-out war was inevitable and the United States would play a vital role in hushing it down.

Maureena and I were spellbound and didn't know what to do. Was it God's indication for her to not go to the Middle East? Or was it His test to see whether we would trust Him in this situation? There was a big decision lying before us, and the choice was completely up to us.

Maureena's placement would be distant from the primarily affected area, but there was no surety of hostilities spilling into nearby countries. There was fear and sadness, and yet a comforting peace upon our lives. We had godly counsel and spent time in prayer concerning her relocation to the Middle East. It was determined: she would be leaving for the Middle East in a month.[8]

By the end of September, Maureena resigned from her services at the Christian Medical College and we boarded a train to Delhi. We hardly talked along the way as we were filled with sadness about our coming separation. I will never forget driving to the airport that night—it was extremely difficult. After arriving in Delhi, Maureena got all the documents and airline tickets from the agency and went to board Gulf Air to proceed to the Middle East.

We said our farewells with choking voices and tearful eyes, hugging and kissing each other. We dared not turn back to look at each other as Maureena went into the check-in lounge. I returned to Ludhiana by the next train in the morning. Throughout the journey, I was soaked in tears and wept erratically. It was unbelievable that though we were emotionally one mind and spirit, our journey of physical separation had begun and we had no idea when it would end. It seemed to be the beginning of an unanticipated nightmare.

I arrived at home but had no idea of Maureena's whereabouts and could only trust God for her safety. The absence of a good telephone network made immediate communication difficult.

After a couple of days, I received a call from Maureena at my workplace. She had arrived in the capital and was transported to an interior region of that country. She sounded tired but was starting to get the hang of things. She gave me a phone number so that I could call on certain days of the week and during emergencies. The phone call was hard as we both wept and couldn't continue talking.

As the days passed, we communicated through letters and once a month we talked on the phone. I moved back to my parental home and continued to teach and supervise at the Catholic school. Maureena was getting acquainted to her new workplace and situation. As usual, it was not long before she was in the groove of things and was making a mark in her profession. Slowly but steadily 1990 was coming to an end.

In the meantime, on the international front, the Middle East crisis was dwindling. The initial conflict to expel Iraqi troops from Kuwait began with an aerial bombardment on January 17, 1991, followed by a ground assault on February 23. It was a decisive victory for the coalition forces, which liberated Kuwait and advanced into Iraqi territory. The coalition ceased their advance and declared a ceasefire 100 hours after the ground campaign started. Aerial and ground combat was confined to Iraq, Kuwait, and areas on the border of Saudi Arabia as I daily watched the war being broadcast on an Indian television station.[9]

As soon as the war began, my family began to worry because Maureena was stationed quite close to the war zone. It would be difficult for anyone to fly in or out. We had to stick to our guns, however, and stay put.

After a couple of sleepless nights, I received a phone call from her. She was apparently doing well and there seemed to be no threat in their region. Knowing the unstable and volatile situation in the Middle East, I knew that any problematic incident could happen there at any time. I didn't show any fearfulness but told her that she could return to India if she sensed a threatening situation.

After talking with her and finding out how she was doing, I planned to visit her parents and tell them how she was doing. While driving my scooter to her parents' home, I had an accident while trying to miss a woman who was crossing the street carrying fodder on her head. I put on the brakes, screeched, and flew out of my seat. Because I was wearing a helmet, I didn't hit my head directly on the pavement, but I was injured nevertheless. Some of our neighbors passing by saw me and brought me home. I was not a good sight, and it took a couple of days for my wounds to heal. My parents nurtured me and took care of my injuries.

I recovered after a week and was then able to give information to Maureena's parents about her welfare. It was about a month later when I was able to tell Maureena about my accident—I knew it would bother her and take her a long time to process it. But apparently, telling her after a long period of time made things much better. She took it with ease.

After Maureena left for the Middle East, I stopped tutoring kids and started to concentrate on higher studies. In 1986, after I gave my graduate exams in sociology and social anthropology, I got through the written exam and interview for doing doctorate studies at Jawaharlal Nehru University (JNU), Delhi. Unfortunately, I couldn't pursue doctorate studies there as my graduate grades were delayed due to the late exams, and JNU had its own deadlines for grade submissions.

I finally received admission for a doctorate in rural sociology at Punjab Agricultural University, Ludhiana. But after continuing these studies for a month, I dropped out due to continual professional harassment from a contending professor. I later opted to do doctorate studies in medical sociology from Punjabi

University, Patiala. I would go out every evening to visit the local doctors and surgeons so that I could gather primary data for compiling my doctorate thesis. It was going very well and I was determined to complete my part-time doctorate studies by 1992.

In the meantime, Maureena had been working hard as a senior nurse for the federal government in the Middle East, occasionally sending me money so that we could build up our bank balance in India for future investments. Things were moving just fine and we had no complaints but praised God for everything He had done in our lives. Even though things were moving fine, they were moving at a slower pace, but almost just as planned.

My work at school was going well. I had a good relationship with all the nuns, brothers, and fathers— they gave me more and more responsibilities. Local schools sought after me for cricket commentary, and even the national board for cricket commentary in Chandigarh invited me to audit so that I would be a part of the Indian National Cricket Commentary team. But knowing this would distract me from my studies, I decided to keep my commentary aspirations confined to my school alone.

I took time to reread the letters Maureena wrote to me during our courting days, as well as the letters she wrote while in the Middle East. Whenever I talked to her or received any letters from her, she had so many stories to tell. We were still fearful of what could happen in the Middle East with the war situation being very tender and delicate.

During her time alone in the Middle East, Maureena had both good and bad experiences. At her workplace, one of the Muslim doctors started to harass her and press her for marriage. She reported the matter to the higher authorities, who transferred him to a remote facility in a short amount of time. At the same time, she made very good friends at her hospital, people who actually became her lifelong friends. She was able to share her life, joys, and hurts, even talking with them about her family.

Most of the people at Maureena's workplace loved her and appreciated her work. Being a nurse on the floor and mentoring the younger ones was never a challenge for her. She even did all three shifts at different intervals as and when the hospital demanded—she always set an example for others.

But being all by herself in the Middle East, life was not easy. She lived in an apartment with five other girls who had left their families in India to have a better life back home. They did all their chores together, stayed together, and always kept an eye for each other's welfare.

One day she was introduced to an underground cell group where girls would get together, spend time in prayer, and meditate on God's Word. She met Brother Ebenezer Vijay[10] and Ambu,[11] his wife, who frequently visited these hidden cell groups. Gradually, Maureena developed a strong bond with the cell groups and the Ebenezer Vijay family.

Hearing Brother Ebenezer's messages and interacting with the girls from the cell group helped Maureena grow steadily in the Lord and His Word. As time flew by, she decided to joyfully get water baptized.

During one of Brother Ebenezer's visits, she tearfully expressed her desire for me to come to the Middle East. The Ebenezer Vijay family and the cell group girls started to pray earnestly for this need.

Sometimes these cell group girls would get together and spend the entire night praying and worshiping God. They began having unbelievable experiences and God started to answer each girl's prayer. They were aware that if they were discovered practicing their faith in secret in an Islamic country, it could spiral them into deep trouble—yet they did not relent. They acknowledged that their lives and safety were solely in God's hands.

Many other such cell groups had sprung up in the country and were now going strong. Slowly and steadily these cells groups were becoming a spiritual assembly to be reckoned with. It was becoming evident that God's hand and power resided on these young men and women of faith.

Just as Maureena's faith grew strong, her superiors noticed her profound abilities and dedication to her job. They started to share more of their responsibilities with her, training her for being a potential manager or director for nursing in the future. She started to attend and conduct many work-related seminars and conferences. Her authorities applauded her for her skill and commitment to her work.

At one of these conferences, she was invited to the capital to participate and give her input about certain medical matters. For a young woman to be staying alone and attending the conference at any Holiday Inn in the Middle East can be an overwhelming experience.

While returning back to her room one evening, an Arab male tried to force himself and board the same elevator she was traveling in. It was in vain, but he followed her elevator up the staircase and continued looking for her. Fortunately, she screamed for help and entered the room of one of her colleagues who was also attending the same conference.

Such incidents happen daily all over the world, but to occur in the Middle East means that they will probably go unreported. Even though the hotel authorities were reported, they didn't take it seriously. When the conference was over, she returned to her hospital and continued to do her work faithfully.

Almost six months had lapsed since Maureena had stepped foot in the Middle East. It was time for her to send in her application for the contracted annual free air ticket and vacation. She planned to visit India during the early fall of 1991. Living without her family for so long brought her deep sadness. Seemingly, she had no appetite or encouragement to eat; her health had deteriorated.

Parting for a month from her friends in the cell group would not be easy, but at the same time she had bubbling joy to reunite with me after such a long separation—it had been nine months! During the course of the weeks and months to follow, she had planned to buy all the stuff she deemed important to bring along with her to India, giving her an excuse to be on a shopping spree for the next few months. She was preparing her mind, emotions, and body to take her first vacation home. In all of this, she did not withhold the glory to God for all His abundant provisions and security. He was good and faithful through everything we had been through!

CHAPTER 3

TOGETHER AGAIN

Therefore a man shall leave his father and mother and be joined to his wife, and they shall become one flesh.

Genesis 2:24

Therefore what God has joined together, let not man separate.

Mark 10:9

By the end of 1990, I saw an advertisement in the newspaper that wanted teachers for the Indian embassy schools in the Middle East. Since it was the same country Maureena was in, seeing this encouraged me greatly. I was 100 percent motivated to go, but I was unsure of the working conditions and the board of directors. I already had a good position and reputation at one of the best schools in Ludhiana, but the salary wasn't very attractive. The qualifications and experience requirements for the embassy schools were quite high, but I qualified. If I was offered a teaching position, it would be easy to take it because seeing Maureena was my greatest priority.

So I applied for a teaching position at the middle school. Shortly after, the call for an interview came and I proceeded to Delhi. I was excited and overwhelmed for the interview. I wanted to keep it a surprise for Maureena, so my parents were the only ones who knew of this.

I prayed and sought godly guidance and intervention in this matter. The day for the interview had finally arrived. The three people on the board asked me questions; I thought it went pretty well. But after it was over, I found out there were candidates who had more experience and higher education than I did. Outwardly, there was no hope for me getting this job. God would have to intervene and turn the hearts of the interview board in my favor. I remembered the Scripture that said, "The king's heart is in the hand of the Lord, like the rivers of water; He turns it wherever He wishes" (Proverbs 21:1). To land this job, I needed a miracle.

The next day I returned to Ludhiana discouraged. I continued to pray for God's favor upon my life. More than anything, I tried to forget the interview I went through. It seemed like a dream.

A couple of months passed by, and before I almost forgot about the interview, I receive an unfamiliar letter in the mail. I had landed the teaching position in the Middle East! This was unbelievable and I knew that it could only be through God's hand. It brought tears to my eyes, taking me some time to process the fact that it would not be long before I would rejoin Maureena in the Middle East.

With heaviness in my heart, I told the convent school that I would soon be leaving for the Middle East to pursue teaching and rejoin my wife. When I broke the news to Maureena, she was thrilled and knew God had answered her prayers too. The next few weeks meant packing and winding things up in India. Before Maureena left for the Middle East, we had planned for her to stay overseas for a maximum of two years. I don't know how that would have ever worked out.

In July of 1991, I traveled to Delhi with my brother-in-law Austin and collected my visa and flight documents from the Gulf Air office. Due to some logistics, I was delayed by a day but landed in the Middle East in one piece.

Maureena and her close friend Daisy came to pick me up at the airport. It was an overwhelming reunion, weeping and hugging one another after what seemed an unending period. I hoped time would stand still. I arrived in the Middle East exactly nine months after Maureena's departure. We had no idea of what God had ahead of us. It seemed scary, but above all we knew our lives were in His hands.

The climatic conditions were pretty hot and humid on the Arabian Coast, but it was the first time I ever had air conditioning. It took me a while to get adjusted to this kind of lifestyle. I taught at one of the largest Indian schools in the Middle East—everyone behaved like they were all strangers.

Though we were finally together didn't mean that we lived together. During our early life in the Middle East, Maureena and I had to live separately as she worked about an hour and a half away. We met on the weekends or when Maureena had free days. The weekends when she was not able to visit me, I would usually take a bus or cab to go see her. Life was hard and discouraging, yet hopeful in many ways.

A new Indian school had opened close to where Maureena resided. We were contemplating whether I should move there the following year or she move with me to the capital. We just had to depend and wait on God to lead us through this ordeal too.

I began to feel the sting of my supervisor while at my job. We came from two different parts of India, so our culture and the pronunciation of words and phrases collided. I tried to work on the changes he desired, but the constant nagging and harassment continued. There was no space for grievance, but only to continue striving for what my boss desired. I received a memo from the principal, explaining the vicissitudes they required from my end. I kept working hard on what was articulated to me but it was all in vain. God had other plans.

Within three months, I received a letter from the principal outlining the termination of services and an immediate flight to India. On hearing the news, Maureena was heartbroken and prayed for God's intervention. I went and met the principal and discussed my plight. He was a kind, humble, and understanding man. I learned that he had been pursuing to become a Catholic priest before he got into teaching. Apparently, during his priestly training, he fell in love with a girl and had to elope, dropping out of Catholic seminary in order to get married. Not conforming to the norms of the Catholic Church, he was excommunicated from the faith. So He chose to join the teaching profession and was where he was because of perseverance and hard work. He worked out a plan for me—I would be transferred to the Indian school that was close to where Maureena worked. I was glad this was going to work out, even though it was much different than what I planned.

Within the next few days, I moved to the town where Maureena resided to begin my teaching job. It was not easy to travel an hour in the killing heat every day. The small school was located in a farm and accommodated in a house. The top grade was five but the school had the potential to grow rapidly. I taught English, social studies, mathematics, and Hindi. Because the school was in its first year, the teachers had to improvise and work hard for its success.

While returning home in a cab after picking up groceries from a town in the mountains of the Gulf Coast one day, I got into a conversation with the cabbie. "What is your faith?" he asked me.

"Masihi," I responded.

"How many wives do you have?" he asked.

I laughed and replied, "Only one! Why do you ask?" I realized later that he was serious and was trying to get at something I was unaware of at the moment.

"If you become a Muslim," he said, "you can easily have four wives. You could even take an Arab woman to be one of your wives."

This conversation suddenly turned serious and it became obvious that they were subtle strategies of

Islamic evangelism. The focus was gratification of the flesh and the bait was abundance of legalized sex in a state under Sharia law. This was a way to lure men of other faiths to embrace Islam.

My stop came and he dropped me off. "May Allah's peace be upon you," he said as I got out of the cab.

As the days continued to fly by, Maureena and I began to think of having our own kids. She was specialized as a pediatric nurse and had a great love and passion for kids. I knew that if we had kids of our own, she would go to every extent to love, pamper, and spoil them.

In a short time we realized that it was not working out as planned. My wife and I underwent some medical tests and examinations. The doctors had only one testimony: "There is nothing wrong with you both; it is nature's course and we can only assist but can't create."

Even though I was dead against going in opposition to how God created us, or assisting Him in any way, Maureena opted for hormonal supplements. I did not want her body to undergo any sort of unnatural pressure or trauma—even the thought itself made me nervous. She had seen and consulted some of the best European doctors available and even undergone endoscopic surgery. But nothing worked out.

During one of our visits to India, we traveled south and had many consultations and procedures with a well-known fertility physician. But nothing was working out. We had a deep sadness, but never manifested it in our demeanor. During all this time, God had been telling me that we were not to have any children but focus our lives on tending and feeding His lonely children on earth.

Finally, during one of our visits to India during the late 1990s, our parents pressured us for in vitro fertilization. The procedure was not only an expensive affair, but also emotionally demoralizing and failed miserably. It was time I put my foot down.

God gave me the audacity to tell Maureena, "Why don't you get it? God does not want us to have kids. Knowing you, if we did, our entire passion and focus would be the kids, and our life would just revolve around them. He is a jealous God and doesn't want us to have any other worldly attachments to infringe that space that solely belongs to Him. He desires Himself to be our first love and expects our life to revolve around Him and His children."

My wife got the message loud and clear. She reconciled submissively and heeded to God's difficult call upon our lives. In unison, we yielded to God's call and never underwent any more medical procedures for having a baby.

I connected with Brother Ebenezer and Ambu, regularly attending and assisting in the underground cell worship services. They began to mentor us, and they exemplified what they wanted to pass on and teach us for future ministry.

We developed a strong bond with them, creating trust, faith, and loyalty toward one another. If we don't have this relationship with our ministry team members, then how can we think to have it with God? Working together for a common goal (extending God's kingdom), being mentored, and submitting our lives under their authority assisted in this close-knit, unbreakable life-long relationship.

My job as a teacher was demanding, and I did not get enough time to be passionately involved and committed to Christ for the extension of His kingdom. There was a fire in my bones, but lack of time.

When 1995 came around, we could sense a spirit of antagonism at the Indian school. It had started to bring in new teachers from India and things were not going as they should. We could sense the principal and the board of directors were up to something fishy, but we weren't able to put our finger on it.

During the midterm examinations, some of the students at school had fared miserably. The principal approached me to raise the grades of the kids whose parents were on the board. This act was unfair and inappropriate to the ones who had done really well, and not to mention it contradicted my faith. My conscience wouldn't allow me to proceed with this deed and my uncompromising attitude offended the principal and the board of directors. I knew exactly what was coming my way.

I didn't receive any memo for the next few months, but just before the academic year got over in May, I was handed a termination of services letter. What I feared the most happened, but I knew that standing up for my faith would reap dividends in the future. I was knocked off my feet, but I remembered Paul talking to the Corinthians: "We are hard-pressed on every side, yet not crushed; we are perplexed, but not in despair;

persecuted, but not forsaken; struck down, but not destroyed" (2 Corinthians 4:8–9); and that "God is our refuge and strength, a very pleasant help in trouble" (Psalm 46:1).

When I broke the news to Maureena, she was in tears and could not restrain herself. We tried to console one another and spend time in prayer, seeking godly guidance and intervention. In vain we contacted the local board of directors and the people in the capital for reinstating my services.

This was a time for me to think about my life and bring about needed radical changes. In my early teens, an evangelist and close family friend, Brother P. C. Varghese, had taught me about Christ. Though I knew about Him and could talk the talk, I was not 100 percent convinced that being a "Christian" was anything more than being born into a Christian family.

I heard many testimonies from people who were born again, but they never convinced me to make a commitment to Jesus myself. The way I saw it was that it was easy for people born in "Christian" families to make that decision. It was no big deal, so why all the hype?

But the turning point came when I heard Jonathan Maharaj from the West Indies,[12] who was the main speaker during an evangelical youth camp I attended.[13] Throughout a time of ministry, he shared his testimony of coming to Christ from a staunch priestly Brahmin Hindu background. He had denounced his Hindu faith and embraced the love and saving grace of Jesus Christ.

This man had risked his life to walk with Jesus Christ. So what was holding me back?

The difficulties and persecution he underwent from his family and friends for his newfound faith in Jesus convicted my heart to yield to the beckoning call of Christ. I was not sure what I was doing or fully getting into, but I truly surrendered my life to Christ and was born again at the age of 16 in October 1979.

I also remembered that when I was 14 months old, my digestive tract seemed to be blocked and the surgeons in Delhi had diagnosed me with volvulus. During the 1960s, any related surgery on kids would usually be fatal. After attempting the risky surgery, the pediatricians had no hope for me to live and my parents gave me up for dead. God was getting around with them, because what they held to be so precious was slipping out of their hands. That day they promised God that if I lived, then I would serve Him all the days of my life. Churches all over Delhi prayed for me, and God answered with a miracle.

One thing I will never forget is that each year, after the long winter break, as I proceeded to continue my studies, my grandmother would give me a pep talk. She would say, "Son, don't ever forget that God saved you from death when you were 14 months old, and He has highly favored you above most people in India. You have the privilege to be educated in a place where the sons and daughters of kings, queens, presidents, and sultans study. Surely, His hand is upon you. Don't ever forget the Lord your God."

In the years that followed, I secretly knew that God's hand and call was upon my life, but in desperation I tried to run away from Him. During the course of my life, it was evident that my parents had forgotten the promise they had made before God when I was on my deathbed. The amazing thing was that God had not forgotten their words; He had taken them very seriously, and He was now on the verge of holding them to it.

Brother Ebenezer and Ambu continually encouraged me with the words of the prophet Isaiah throughout this difficult time. Even though God's plan was hard to see at the moment, He still had a plan for me. Isaiah declared:

> "For My thoughts are not your thoughts, nor are your ways My ways," says the Lord. "For as the heavens are higher than the earth, so are My ways higher than your ways, and My thoughts than your thoughts."
>
> Isaiah 55:8–9

We knew something greater was coming our way, and we just had to wait in humility and patience before God to part the Red Sea in our lives. But before He could do that, He desired complete obedience and adherence to His Word. I had to allow the Spirit of God to do His work in my life. The next few months would be the turning point of my life.

With no help in sight for a local Arab to sponsor my stay in the Middle East, we struggled to decide whether to be there or not. After seeking counsel from matured believers in the body of Christ, I took the federal government's written exam and interview for teaching English as a second language. I was relying solely on God's grace to see me through the test. I was assured a potential teaching position at one of the government madrassas[14] on the condition of any hired overseas teacher not filling the vacancy. But no one really knew how long that would take.

I was disheartened the day we traveled to the capital to attempt the federal education exam, but I was desperate to know whether God really wanted us to continue there or not. I remember that summer day while we drove on the winding road, which went through the lonely deserted Arabian mountains. The sky was clear and light blue. There was no chance of rain at this time of the year. Out of nowhere, I saw a tiny cloud and asked God for an impossible sign: "Lord, if You give us rain today, then we stay; but if not, then we will leave immediately."

This seemed difficult to attempt in the natural realm, but I knew that there was nothing impossible for the living God. As we returned home that evening, the sky was overcast with grey clouds. And it rained nonstop. It is common for flash floods to accompany rain in the Middle East. In fact, if one is not vigilant, they can easily be swept into the Arabian Sea.

As expected, the flash floods were in full swing and we got stranded along the way. We stopped our car and shed tears of joy knowing that God had silently given His verdict. While waiting for the flood to recede, Maureena and I spent some time praying and thanking

God for answering our prayer.[15] We didn't know how God would make my stay possible, but we can surely testify that His hand is never shortened.

Sometime later God raised an Arab friend who came beside me and sponsored my stay in the Middle East. But the wait while being unemployed would test my patience. This drove my wife and me to spend more time in prayer and His Word.

So during the next few months, God shut me up in my home. It was quite evident that He wanted to spend more time with me than I had ever spent with Him before—and the desire was equally mutual. This well-spent time taught me to pray, worship God, and be in His Word no matter the circumstances.

This time of unemployment was also a time of growth for me. I became more matured in the faith and developed patience. Even the works of my flesh—specifically anger—were gradually fading away. I became more focused on Christ and braced myself to encounter any unpleasant events in my life.

God had been profoundly working in my life, and I was now at a point where I desired more of Him. With the passing of time, the craving for my Creator intensified, and it seemed that no matter what I did, I was unable to get more of Him.[16] My life was being transformed from the inside out. It was this amazing experience that would firmly establish our steadfast faith in Jesus and solidify the ministry to the body of Christ.

During summer vacation, I started to tutor Arab students in English at a private tutorial center. This lasted till the students had their vacation. So I was back in the four corners of my house, learning to wait on God and His timing. Spending precious hours in the presence of God did me good. The Spirit of God had steered my heart in such a way that I would bear allegiance to Christ and His name alone.

Summer went by and I didn't hear from the federal education office. So I contacted them again during the fall. The authorities at the education office assured me of an opening in the near future, and we were growing hopeful of future job prospects. We couldn't continue like this for long. It was extremely challenging to make ends meet on Maureena's salary alone.

Finally, during one of my prayer times, I set a deadline for God: "If I don't have the federal teaching job by December 31, 1995, Maureena and I are returning to India." We would have to wait for over a month to see whether God took our words seriously or not.

CHAPTER 4

SWEET STRUGGLES

In this you greatly rejoice, though now for a little while, if need be, you have been grieved by various trials, that the genuineness of your faith, being much more precious than gold that perishes, though it is tested by fire, may be found to praise, honor, and glory at the revelation of Jesus Christ.

1 Peter 1:6–7

My brethren, count it all joy when you fall into various trials, knowing that the testing of your faith produces patience. But let patience have its perfect work, that you may be perfect and complete, lacking nothing.

James 1:2–4

As December drew to a close, I received a call from the federal government's education department to start teaching at a location that was far away from where Maureena worked. It would be a challenge, but God knew what He was doing. Because of this, Maureena asked for a transfer not far from where I would be working.

On December 29, 1995—just two days before my deadline—I started to teach English as a second language to middle school boys. I was unaware of being posted at one of the most dreadful and undisciplined schools of that region.

The madrassa was right on the coast, and while teaching we would experience the hot, humid air bear the fragrance of drying fish and the salty ocean. Despite the location and environment being not conducive for teaching or learning, we did what was expected of us. I earned double the salary of what I got at my previous school and had ample free time to do whatever I desired.

Besides other Arab teachers from different countries, I was the only Indian and Christian teacher at this school. During my free classes and break times, many colleagues would ask me questions about my faith. God gave me the grace and boldness to stand up to any queries or intimidating questions. I continually reflected on the passage Paul wrote to Timothy: "For God has not given us a spirit of fear, but of power and of love and of a sound mind" (2 Timothy 1:7). Prayerfully meditating on this biblical text kept me strong in the midst of people who were repulsed by my faith in Christ.

Being directly connected to the Arab people—their faith and culture—I had to learn many things. First, I placed effort in learning the Arabic language. The best place to pick it up was from the streets, talking to kids who knew nothing but Arabic. Observing their behavior and culture assisted me in understanding them as a people and being able to connect with them more easily.

Many foreign teachers became my friends and wanted to learn more about my country, faith, and culture. I started to connect with many of the kids from the student body. As I had no books or materials to help, it was much simpler to learn to live in an Arab community from one's experience and pitfalls.

As discipline and controlling students are some of the major problems of the boys' schools in the Arab world, some of my colleagues wanted to teach me the skills and techniques of creating a profound impression and be able to regulate my class with ease. During the school session every day, they advised me to always have an angry demeanor, which would make the students fear me and cause them to stay disciplined. They also believed if students still behaved in an unruly manner, then the teacher must pick out one of the weak boys and give him a thorough thrashing so that fear was created amongst the pupils, gaining their respect. These teachers were experienced and knew the name of the game in teaching boys in the Middle East.

As expected, I did not adhere to their counsel but depended on God's grace and protection upon my life. Students were disciplined and desired to be taught in my class, and my supervisors and principal were satisfied. By God's grace and mercy, I had accomplished what I thought was a mighty mountain to surpass.

One of the things I learned during my teaching career here was that in Islamic countries, people usually recognize you by your faith and not by your name. On meeting any new person of Asian descent, they would first ask about my faith rather than my name.

On knowing my faith, they would then decide whether to converse with me or not; and if so, what kind of conversation to have. This is just the way the Arab mind worked, and I had to get used to it.

One of the questions that continually came up when asked about my faith was, "As you are living in the Arab world, why are you still a Christian and not a Muslim?"

I would normally answer by saying, "I am not just a Christian, but a practicing Christian." This answer would usually get their attention because they had never encountered such an answer before. It would give way to a long conversation where I had the opportunity to share my faith in Christ and frequently have the last word by casually inviting them to experience what I experienced.

Another question I frequently encountered was, "Are you a slave?"

My answer would always be, "Yes, I am. I'm a slave to Christ, to whom I bear my allegiance and owe my life." I would do this while considering the apostle Paul's words, "For he who is called in the Lord while a slave is the Lord's freedman. Likewise he who is called while free is Christ's slave" (1 Corinthians 7:22). This answer would trigger a series of questions where they would be more inquisitive about my faith in Christ. This gave me the opportunity to tell them what Christ has done for me and what He has already done for them.

These discussions showed me that they didn't consider the sacrifice on the cross too highly—for them, it was a weak effort on God's part. Some even considered this act of Christ a farce, so-called Christian propaganda. This provoked me to study the Qur'an and apprehend what their scriptures had to say for refuting the deity of Christ and negating Him as the God-Man.

My stay at this school was for five short months, but I got the experience I would need for years to come. I wasted a lot of time and gas on traveling back and forth for one and a half hours a day. I eventually asked for another transfer to the vicinity where my wife worked.

So in the summer of 1996, I was transferred to another coastal school in the same region where Maureena worked. Things became much simpler for us, our workplaces were close and I had more time to myself as I was just expected to work 25 hours a week.

My wife and I were gradually getting more involved in underground ministry with Brother Ebenezer and Ambu. I was still teaching at a middle school for boys and having the same daily routine. At one of the parent-teacher meetings, I happen to meet the sheikh of the adjoining village. I had no idea I taught his son, who was really impressed with me as a teacher. The sheikh wanted to meet me in order to put a face to the teacher his son constantly talked about. The conversation that followed was interesting.

The sheikh had many stories to tell, most notably how he spent his youth and early adulthood serving the military folks from the West while they resided in the Middle East. I could see that he was inquisitive to know about my faith, so I didn't shrink back. He asked me whether the Garden of Eden was the same as Aden of Yemen. Politely, I mentioned that it was not so and invited him to have the "JESUS" movie and the Bible in Arabic to get a better perspective of Jesus Christ and Christianity. I was taking a long leap of uncertainty, believing in Christ to move his heart and, at the same time, lifting a prayer of faith to God. After a quick pause, he agreed to accept the "JESUS" film and the Arabic Bible.

The next week I handed over the Arabic Bible and "JESUS" movie to the sheikh's son so he could give it to his dad. After a couple of months, the sheikh showed up at the school and asked for me. I certainly didn't expect to get into another discussion with him about faith. He had come to give me his verdict.

He confidently told me that the "JESUS" movie was trash and the Bible was polluted. On hearing that statement, it caused me to burn from within. God was teaching me patience and causing the fruit of the Holy Spirit to grow. I simply listened to his false accusations of my Lord. How was this possible?

I was immediately reminded of Jesus's words: "But I say to you, love your enemies, bless those who curse you, do good to those who hate you, and pray for those who spitefully use you and persecute you" (Matthew 5:44). I began to pray for God to save the sheikh...if not, then I prayed God would allow others at his home to get access to this movie and Bible, and possibly be saved in the process.

My tenure at this school lasted for only a year when the head office asked me to start teaching at the secondary level. I was transferred to a school that was in our neighborhood, and my wife managed the health center that was right next door. It was quite evident that God was about to do something that we were not expecting.

While getting my car washed one day, I met an Afghan worker named Javed, who drove semis for a local Arab trader. We got into an interesting conversation when I asked him, "How did you come to the Middle East?"

"The local wars of different factions and the Russian invasion had compelled me and my family to leave Afghanistan," he said. "Many of my brothers and cousins are here too, but I lost a number of my family during the civil war."

I invited him to come to my home and spend some time with me whenever he had the opportunity. I would also meet him every now and then when I went downtown. He came to my home a couple of times and shared his family struggles and job problems. And whenever his wife and children had medical issues, he would bring them to the hospital where Maureena would lovingly take care of them.

His wife talked very softly and was always clad in a burkha,[17] while his kids seemed fearful of everyone they met. Maureena had to be extra loving, tender, and sensitive to their needs.

No sooner had we befriended an Afghan family and had built up strong ties with them, that I slowly started to share the love of Christ with Javed, who was all ears to this new gospel but had long known Christ as the Great Prophet. Our conversations were more centered on Issa Masih than anything else.

Whenever he traveled to the capital or to a different country, Javed would get me stuff that was not available in our location. He would even drop us off at the airport whenever we went overseas and pick us up on our return. He and his family had become our faithful friends till one day he told me, "My employer has employed one of his family members to drive the semis, and now my family and I have to return to Afghanistan within a week."

Our hearts broke as I did not know what to do for him—my hands were tied in a nation that was not our own. His life taught me how to be faithful and loyal to one's friends even if it means giving up your life for them.

CHAPTER 5

GETTING INVOLVED

Who shall separate us from the love of Christ?
Shall tribulation, or distress, or persecution, or
famine, or nakedness, or peril, or sword? As it
is written: "For Your sake we are killed all day
long; we are accounted as sheep for the slaughter." Yet in all these things we are more than
conquerors through Him who loved us. For I
am persuaded that neither death nor life, nor
angels nor principalities nor powers, nor things
present nor things to come, nor height nor
depth, nor any other created thing, shall be able
to separate us from the love of God which is in
Christ Jesus our Lord.

Romans 8:35–39

Be diligent to present yourself approved to God,
a worker who does not need to be ashamed,
rightly dividing the word of truth.

2 Timothy 2:15

God began to push us to get involved in ministry to the
dormant body of Christ on the Arabian Coast. After
testing our hearts and having a first-hand glimpse of

our lives, Brother Ebenezer and Ambu invited us to join them in ministering in the coastal region. We would look for potential opportunities to plant underground churches in the Middle East and continue to keep the ones that already existed running.

My wife and I were now on the road to become "underground tentmakers." The term referred to a method of Christian evangelism in which missionaries support themselves by working full time in the marketplace with their skills and education, instead of receiving financial support from a church or ministry.

Pastors, ministers, evangelists, and Christian workers are unwelcome to come and radically practice their faith or lead others to it in most of the Islamic world. Building places of worship other than mosques are completely prohibited; therefore, a generation of "underground tentmakers" still exists in the Middle East. God prepared us under the mentorship of Brother Ebenezer and his wife to take on the ministerial challenges that the underground church faces in the Middle East.

Our jobs were going well and our supervisors always appreciated us, which was an enormous encouragement for both of us. We needed to glorify and exemplify Christ at our workplaces. But ministerial opportunities had started to come fast. We were immediately assigned to manage three underground churches. The one where Maureena took Sunday school and I handled the youth was very close to a major naval base. Many nonlocals from different Asian countries attended the services there.

When Brother Ebenezer asked me to preach my first sermon there, I did it out of reluctance. I still remember the topic was "salvation," and the Scripture text was Genesis 6:13–7:16. The parallel of Noah and the flood took form with God's salvation and baptism for us through Christ. I believe it was God's amazing grace that it hit the target that was intended. Brother Ebenezer asked me to preach the same message in many other underground meetings. And wherever people heard it, they were blessed.

I remember Brother Ebenezer giving altar calls after the message, to which many responded positively. I had no idea of the profound impact God's Word could have on the lives of people. I saw what the writer of Hebrews stated: "For the word of God is living and powerful, and sharper than any two-edged sword, piercing even to the division of soul and spirit, and of joints and marrow, and is a discerner of the thoughts and intents of the heart" (Hebrews 4:12). Surely our God is an awesome God and He can do what no man can even dream of doing.

A new family began to attend one of our meetings on the coast. The young lady was a Hindu and was excited to be there because of the stories she had learned from her kids who had been coming to our Sunday school.[18] During the course of the next few months, she claimed she was being delivered and blessed, and wanted the same experience for her husband as well. He was a Catholic and given up to menial jobs and drinking a lot at night. He would occasionally be violent and abusive to his wife and two lovely kids.

So his family dragged him to one of our meetings. Though we didn't come from the same part of India, we still connected pretty well. I learned that he played the keyboard, so I invited him to play it during our singing and praise time. All his life he played on secular bands and had never led any type of church worship. It was evident from his lifestyle that he had not surrendered his life to Christ.

He initially came to our meetings half-heartedly, and it took him some time to get acquainted with worshiping the living God. It was really hard to mentor and teach him, but with patience it was not impossible. It was a bumpy ride, but well worth it.

After midnight one night, we received a call from this Hindu lady, telling us that her husband had come home drunk and was abusive to the family so she locked him out. That apparently didn't deter him to continue pounding at the door. We traveled 20 minutes to get there and help resolve their family issues.

The next time the family showed up for the underground cell meeting, they seemed to be on their best behavior, but it was evident from their body language that everything wasn't going as it seemed. Maureena and I sat down with the family to counsel and assist them in getting their lives in order.

Sometime later, we invited them to surrender their lives to Christ and be born again. What amazed us was that both of them accepted the offer and were willing to look over their past and lead a brand new life for Christ. What a joy it was for the body of Christ! We were concerned about them getting into any kind of tussle that would take them on the same path again. It was encouraging to see that they adhered to the biblical advice Paul addressed to married Christians: "Wives, submit to your own husbands, as is fitting in the Lord. Husbands, love your wives and do not be bitter toward them" (Colossians 3:18–19).

Even though God was working powerfully among us, Maureena and I didn't feel safe, as people living nearby would often steal from us or break into our car. So we moved yet again to another location along the coast. This was a single family home with our own well and high-rise walls surrounding it. A doctor lived next door, so we felt quite safe there.

One spring day after one of our big trips to visit some friends at a distant location, we resumed our weekly routine and jobs. I came home after work and found the back door of our home wide open, and one of the AC vents in the wall was ripped out. I thought Maureena had come by and left it like this. So I looked for our valuable belongings—they were all gone. All of our gold, cash, and our high-end camera were missing. It was quite evident that we had been robbed.

I called Maureena, Ebenezer, and Ambu, and we informed the police immediately. Within minutes I picked up my wife from work and the police were on their way. They came with dogs and tried to investigate and locate the thief. Apparently, all the drama that transpired was in vain. No evidence was found and no suspect was located or interrogated. Brother Ebenezer and Ambu showed up in the afternoon and had great concern for our safety and occurrence of future events like this. We were in shock and didn't know how to handle such a situation. They spent a couple of hours with us, and we also got some time to pray and discuss important matters.

That evening I got a hold of some Afghan construction workers and got the destroyed air conditioning vent repaired permanently. They were good-hearted guys and never asked me for a penny. In fact, when I offered them money, they turned it down. My wife prepared food and fed them with a sumptuous meal before they left. At the end of the day, we learned that "in everything give thanks; for this is the will of God in Christ Jesus for you" (1 Thessalonians 5:18). We praised God for losing only our valued possessions— we could have been killed if the intruders would have come at night. And being killed in a foreign Islamic land, we could easily be forgotten and our lives not accounted for. We thanked God for sparing our lives.

With all of the ministerial responsibilities we had been given, it made it difficult to annually travel to India. So we tried to make a trip every two to three years. But each time we went to India, we returned back to the Middle East discouraged, disappointed, and spiritually demoralized. Without fail we were at a standstill with my parents who continually pestered us to return back to India. But we would not move till God would give us direction in the matter.

Not being able to give up the Lord's work in lieu of my parents brought us to a point of contention with them. They also started to pressure us to adopt a child, which a number of people in our family and circle of friends had already articulated to us. Though I had reminded Maureena of God's instructions to us in this matter, she went ahead with pursuing how to make this come to fruition. She went to every length and breadth to procure a child for us. I could just imagine why Sarah was so desperate to have a kid that she even shared her husband with her maid (Genesis 16:2)!

This was mind-boggling to me—not following God's instructions could easily get us into deep trouble. The truth is that Sarah didn't realize that some five thousand years down the line, her choice would get the world into a big hole. I stayed firm on godly instructions and obedience, but Maureena listened to those familiar voices. Pondering the biblical truths and contemporary examples, I knew falling prey to ungodly voices would only result in giving us a bad taste in our mouths for ages to come.

Some of our family and friends advised us to adopt from a children's home or embrace an orphan. Apparently, some of them, who had a longing heart for us, went to the extent of becoming pregnant themselves and designated that the growing child in their womb would be ours. This went on in succession at different intervals during the course of seven years with seven different families volunteering to accomplish what we could not achieve. They were on a serious mission to assist God in something they thought was more important to us than really listening to what God desired of us. Unfortunately, all seven babies died. Some died in the womb, a couple were stillborn, and a few died after some hours of their births. I believe God was more serious than we thought about this issue. His message was loud and clear.

My wife and I sat down and had a heart-to-heart conversation about the past incidences when Maureena argued that God had not said no to adoption. I had to rebuttal and make it very clear that His instructions in the past had been obvious: we were not to have children. This, of course, meant that we were not to have children from any source—natural born, adopted, orphans, etc. The only thing missing in this instruction was our voluntary submission to be obedient to the word He had given us. From that day forward, though my wife may secretly desire to have kids, she has never mentioned pursuing having kids of our own again.

When the natural realm overshadows us and our human instincts are triggered, we yearn and desire to have kids of our own—someone who would bear our name and we could call our very own. I know this desire will not fade away but become overtly distinct with the passing of years. We only pray that God will continually give us His grace and unfailing strength to help us overcome this natural desire.

Deep down in our hearts, we knew these tests, struggles, and scars would be the building blocks of our maturity and ministry for Christ. God was preparing and gearing us up for greater and harder things yet to come.

CHAPTER 6

MAKING OF TENTMAKERS

Did I commit sin in humbling myself that you might be exalted, because I preached the gospel of God to you free of charge?... And in everything I kept myself from being burdensome to you, and so I will keep myself.

2 Corinthians 11:7, 9

But you be watchful in all things, endure afflictions, do the work of an evangelist, fulfill your ministry.

2 Timothy 4:5

Even though Maureena and I are not perfect in God's sight, He began using untalented and insignificant people like us for His glory. This was because we were available and had a heart to submit, obey, follow, and adhere to His Word. Above all else, He knew that we would not rely on our own strength or wisdom, but be completely dependent upon Him for extending His kingdom.

I cannot fathom why God trusted us to care and shepherd His flock. This has always overwhelmed us as we put all our effort in staying faithful and obedient to His call. I remember the call and hand of God upon my life from birth, but I had run away from it during my teens and early twenties. God desired me to be His servant, and I had completely ignored it. I decided it wasn't my work to share His Word or extend His kingdom, but it was the assignment He had entrusted to pastors, preachers, and evangelists.

In order to break me, shaping me to do His will, He brought Maureena and I to the Middle East. God had raised a small band of tentmakers who would secretly, without fearing persecution, jail time, deportation, or even death, extended His kingdom throughout that area. God patiently waited for me to voluntarily come around. He brought us to the place where we would realize that it was no time to stand on the sidelines but jump into the game. It was evident from the testimonies of Brother Ebenezer, others in the body of Christ, and our personal experiences, that our yielding and adherence to God's call was generating drastic transformation in our lives, behavior, and character.

The walk on water had begun. We were now witnessing the underground ministry starting to develop. Throughout the entire week we would conduct four underground meetings on the coast at different undisclosed locations. Many non-Christians, Hindus, Buddhists, Sikhs, Muslims, Catholics, and even atheists had started to come. Men, women, and children of Asian and African descent began to explore these underground cell groups as well.

At one of the weekly meetings, we would minister only to ladies with some men showing up occasionally.

Whenever we arrived for this meeting, a reluctant gentleman would try to sneak out, telling us that there was something more important he had to attend to. This went on for some time until we demonstrated concern for his life and strongly encouraged him to attend the meetings.

The next time we had the meeting, he was there again. But he was apparently reluctant to continue. We continued to pursue him and let him know we were concerned about his life. When he started facing problems a couple months later, he showed up again. But this time he was not leaving. In the days that followed, his life turned around and he became a brand new person. Today, he fervently serves the underground church.

At the same cell group, there was a lady who held a prestigious office in the medical field. Though she was a chatterbox, she was serious about God. There were some drastic changes taking place in her life. You could see humility and grace flooding her life.

During the worship time at one of the meetings, she started to weep and pray passionately. She asked God to bring about hard tests and trials in her life so that she would be drawn to Him more intimately. Her yearning was for the undesirable. I had never heard anyone pray that prayer before.

The group meeting that day was taken by surprise, and everyone was in tears by the time worship was over. She didn't realize that the next few months were going to be the hardest she had ever faced. She now faced persecution from her superiors, and within a matter of months she resigned from her job and left to take care of her family in India, where we regularly received news from her. She was now being persecuted in her own home. During this time of testing and trials, she testified that she had been growing in the Lord but never had she experienced this kind of freedom and closeness to God.

We lost a spot for conducting one of our meetings on the coast. Believers in that area were perplexed and desperately needed a place to worship. A family offered their small home and we continued to have our underground meetings there. Unfortunately, it didn't last long as that family planned to return to India the following year. We were standing at the same place where we were just a couple of years ago.

We were in a dilemma—no one was willing to open their home. It was probably out of fear, a lack of space, or even the poor location and structure of their homes, but that didn't really matter for anyone in that group. Finally, a Hindu couple at one of the schools learned about this issue and offered to open their home at night. All of us were excited to meet at this middle-aged couple's home.

We continued to meet there for over a year when the unexpected happened. The couple started to question their faith in their Hindu gods. They got interested in what was going on during these underground meetings.

During the days that followed, the man of the house contracted a tumor in his abdomen. We could only pray, encourage, and assure them that our God is the only living God who can heal. Without fail, the cell group continued to pray fervently. The surgeons at the general hospital had set a date for his surgery. I happened to be in the city that week conducting secondary examinations, so I decided to visit him.

When I saw him, I laid hands on his abdomen, and prayed for God to manifest Himself as Yahweh Rapha, our Healer. I was crying out in the Spirit for healing. Before he was wheeled into the operation room the next day, the doctors came over to his room for a final checkup. They could not feel any tumor in his abdomen at all! Confused and baffled, they took him for a final scan. "Where did the visible tumor go?" they asked.

They frantically searched and compared the older scans to the new one. Everything was crystal clear. There was no tumor! The church knew exactly what happened to it. We all prayed and God had answered just in the nick of time.

I informed Brother Ebenezer, all the cell group members, and believers at other locations, and there was great joy and celebration in the body of Christ for the God we adore and worship. After this Hindu man was healed, his faith in idols started to dwindle and he and his wife came to a point of complete acceptance and surrender to the living God. Two more souls were added to the kingdom of God that day. He was doing unbelievable things on the coast and we were privileged to bear witness to His great works.

No sooner we learned that a ship would be docking at the main harbor and, if anyone was interested, they could host any of the crew on board. My wife and I were up for the challenge. We could receive a call at any time—night or day—to pick up the couple that would be staying with us. It took a couple of days before they were permitted to dock and enter the country, but then the call came.

So Maureena and I drove to the capital one night to pick them up. They were a young couple from Michigan around our age and had voluntarily decided before God that they would not have kids till they had faithfully fulfilled the assignment of reaching out to the different countries they stopped at during their voyage. Before we went home that night, they gave us a tour of their humungous ship. It was a great privilege, honor, and joy for us to host a man and a woman of God who were passionate and had taken many risks for Christ during their journey.

We drove them around to see and preach at the different underground cell groups. They told their stories by integrating them with biblical ones and had a lot of fun with the Sunday school kids at one of our locations. It was amazing to see that their bodies were immune to extreme temperatures and foods from different countries. Spices and peppers did not really bother them either, and they relished in whatever was laid on the table. We had taken them out twice to see the dry desert, rugged mountains, ancient forts, and even the springs in the wilderness.

It was an amazing week as they ministered to our souls through God's Word and their personal testimonies. It is incredible to see how people who are sold out to God can camouflage themselves to get into closed countries for short-term missions. They were truly used by God for the small amount of time they were here.

Maureena and I used to have late night church during the weekend at one of our other locations. This was designed to cater to the needs of all those who got off work late. Even though a couple of them would doze off during the service, they just wanted to be there, being refreshed in God's presence.

What astonished me the most upon arriving was that the room overflowed with people who were hungry and desperate for God. Many times I would be overwhelmed to see their genuine passion for their Savior. It was mind-blowing to watch them passionately worship God in spirit and in truth. Sitting in His presence, one could never be oblivious to the power and stirring of the Holy Spirit.

A Hindu gentleman who worked at a nearby pharmacy was facing some critical issues in his life. So one of his friends told him to come to our meetings. Restraining himself from talking to others, he started to attend these meeting regularly. He liked what he heard, and his soul was being convicted and stirred to examine his own faith in his gods. He had hard discussions with my mentor and me regarding our faith in Jesus Christ.

One thing I recall telling him was that my own forefathers were Hindus and my grandparents had embraced Christ and given up their idols. They came to Christ through some American missionaries who had come to India during the early 1900s. They made their choice, realizing that what Christ did for them no one had done before and would never do again.

I also explained that every person who dedicates themselves as a god has a tomb or shrine set up for them, whereas Jesus was the only resurrected One, separating Him from all the others. If Christ died and had not been resurrected, He would just be like everyone else. Our faith in Christ stood out because He proved who He really was, is, and will continue to be.

As the days passed by, the Hindu pharmacist's heart was drawn to Christ. And the day finally came when he completely surrendered his life to Jesus. He was born again! He gradually grew in the Lord and the day finally came when I handed over the responsibility of this cell group to him and ventured out to plant others. The last I heard of him was that he had returned to South India and was going from village to village on a bicycle, evangelizing by proclaiming the gospel of Christ.

When this gentleman left the shores of India as a Hindu to fend for work in the Middle East, did he ever think in his wildest dreams that he would one day return to be a missionary for Jesus Christ? It was so encouraging for us to hear that God had raised and shaped one soul from our cell group to be a missionary in his own homeland. God was truly at work in our midst.

CHAPTER 7

MEETING GOD'S SMUGGLER

"No weapon formed against you shall prosper, and every tongue which rises against you in judgment you shall condemn. This is the heritage of the servants of the Lord, and their righteousness is from Me," says the Lord.

Isaiah 54:17

But you shall receive power when the Holy Spirit has come upon you; and you shall be witnesses to Me in Jerusalem, and in all Judea and Samaria, and to the end of the earth.

Acts 1:8

Brother Ebenezer asked Maureena and I to meet him and his wife, Ambu, at one of the locations of a temporary cell group as they had an interesting surprise waiting for us. On our arrival that evening, we got the opportunity to meet and hear the well-known "God's Smuggler."

He dreamed of being a spy undercover behind enemy lines when he was just a boy. As a man he found himself working undercover for God. For decades his life story, recounted in God's Smuggler, has awed and inspired millions of people. I read his book and captivating evangelism stories a number of years ago. He smuggled Bibles and Christian material into Communist China and parts of the Middle East. We now had the great privilege and honor of meeting him in person.

Meeting a president of any country would be an honor for us, but meeting such people as God's smuggler was truly extraordinary. It made our day. We had a couple of hours to spend with him and learn about evangelical operations in hard and stiff countries where Christian literature is not only banned, but Christians are persecuted and even killed for promulgating their faith in any form.

Secret evangelism is dangerous, but also has its own rewards. One should never step into any kind of Christian ministry till they clearly and audibly hear it from God Himself, let alone ministry in nations that are closed off and even hostile to God. It is a serious affair as one has to daily put their life on the line, not knowing if they will be caught or killed that day. There is no space for mess-ups or dabbling with God's Word.

When a person is on the move in underground ministry, it causes the adrenaline to rush, making them susceptible to vulnerability and error. Therefore, a person has to be very focused, goal-oriented, obedient to God, biblically sound, and walking and moving in the power of the Holy Spirit. It is also important to have integrity and give yourself to a lifestyle of prayer and fasting. Depending on God and being obedient to Him is life or death in some countries.

God's smuggler told us about one of his trips into the northern part of the Arabian Peninsula. He had walked into an airport where the authorities would trash Bibles or any Christian material they could lay hands on. As he was bringing in a massive container packed with Arabic and English pocket Bibles and tracts, the gentleman at the immigration counter asked for his passport and entry documents, which he gladly handed over. But on asking about his luggage, God's smuggler said he had a large container of Christian material.

He was obviously not allowed to enter the country with such material, even facing a jail sentence for bringing in such a humungous case. Fearlessly, God's smuggler said that he would wait till the package would be allowed to go with him. In the meantime, he prayed for God's leading and intervention. Back in his own country, he had a lot of faithful intercessors that continually supported him through prayer whenever he was on trips. They were surely praying now.

God's smuggler then saw a sheikh and his entourage land at the airport. As he was about to exit, God's smuggler approached him and told him about his confiscated package and its contents—he was treading on one of the most dangerous places with this container of Christian literature and Bibles. The sheikh signaled with his hand to the man in charge, and customs released the package to him and he went on his way.

The God who made a way through the Red Sea for the Israelites is the same yesterday, today, and forever. He is a God of all impossibilities and His hand is never shortened. God answered his prayer in a powerful way. He didn't leave him nor did He forsake him.

God's smuggler went on his way to get the literature in the hands of the right people to quickly distribute it throughout that country. It was a ray of hope for many and quenched the thirst of the longing, parched souls. God had done the unexpected and He alone was entitled to receive the glory!

Sometime later, God gave Brother Ebenezer the opportunity to host a visiting evangelical team from Texas. It was a God-ordained time where we learned to move in the power of the Holy Spirit, manifesting the profound gifts of discernment, knowledge, and truth.

The team ministered to a number of leaders in the underground cell groups, and a couple of them experienced breakthroughs in their lives. As time went by, this renewal meeting motivated us to initiate night vigils at different locations throughout the coast. To see how it would work, we started bi-monthly vigils during weekends and then introduced another vigil in a town close to the mountains. Most of the people would come after they had prepared themselves with fasting.

The meetings would usually begin around 10 p.m. with exuberant praise and worship, delving into occasional prayer with interludes of praise. Someone would sporadically share a passage from God's Word, or a testimony or two. This phenomenon would engage all the attendees, encouraging them to indulge in more praise and worship to the King of all kings and Lord of all lords. There were also intervals for eating and drinking (if all were not fasting), and even a short chat.

But things really got exciting after 2 a.m. I don't know why, but I think that the lengthy time of praise and worship apparently created an atmosphere for the manifestation and operation of the gifts of the Holy Spirit. Many were healed and prophesied over. One would witness the operation of the gifts of discernment and words of knowledge, and another would operate in the gift of tongues and the interpretation of tongues. This was just the beginning of events where many untold stories of transformation and yearning for God emerged.

We encountered what the first church in Acts 2 experienced:

> When the Day of Pentecost had fully come, they were all with one accord in one place. And suddenly there came a sound from heaven, as of a rushing mighty wind, and it filled the whole house where they were sitting. Then there appeared to them divided tongues, as of fire, and one sat upon each of them. And they were all filled with the Holy Spirit and began to speak with other tongues, as the Spirit gave them utterance.
>
> Acts 2:1–4

Our meetings would usually wind down by about 6 a.m., but we would leave for our homes half-heartedly desiring more of God's awesome presence.

During the Eid holidays[19] that year, we made the most overwhelming trip of our life. We traveled to the Ophir region[20] of the Middle East and stayed there for a week. The prodigious drive through the desert in the fall was exciting and an experience in itself. We got to see the idle harbor where the Queen of Sheeba had anchored her ships while visiting Solomon in all his grandeur. We also got to meet the beautiful coffee-skinned tribe people with black, piercing eyes,[21] who were presumably the descendants of Job; and the hazel-eyed, light-skinned progenies of Abraham and Keturah.

Our visit to the tomb of the prophet Ayub (Job) just swept us of our feet. We spent a couple hours walking around in reverence there, reflecting on his writings. We shed tears while alluding to his sufferings and the glorious outcome of his life. It was a truly wonderful time.

Our final destination was an excursion to the mountains of Ophir, which were known for gold mining in the past. This is where we explored the woods and extracted frankincense and myrrh from the trees. It seemed like we had visited the Old Testament in perspective, and the thirst of our soul to walk and breathe the same air our forefathers did was quenched.

While returning, we stopped at a health center and, at the prompts of the residents there, we had church in the bedroom of one of the staff members—a secret mini-revival meeting of ten people! This is what we needed to top off our trip.

In order to protect this territory from dirt, filth, and other not so honorable infiltrations, most of the countries in the Middle East are closed to second- or third-class tourism. One can only get a glimpse of European or American tourists enjoying the lush land.

During one of our land exploration tours, we happened to bump into some European tourists and got into a conversation that completely bewildered us. In the course of the conversation we learned they were believers, so we could identify with them easily. This couple had come to this land for the sole purpose of walking, driving, and climbing the land to claim it for Christ. They claimed the promise that God had given to Moses, Joshua, and the children of Israel: "Every place that the sole of your foot will tread upon I have given you, as I said to Moses" (Joshua 1:3). Needless to say, this was not the last time we would meet them.

God was up to something new in that nation. In times to come, we would involve this couple and many like them to ignite the passion and fire amongst those who were part of the underground church, turning the hearts and claiming the inhabitants of this land for Christ. Through meeting God's smuggler and seeing what God was doing in our midst, courage was arising within our souls to continue the work God had called us to.

CHAPTER 8

UNDERGROUND CHURCHES

But the hour is coming, and now is, when the true worshipers will worship the Father in spirit and truth; for the Father is seeking such to worship Him.

John 4:23

And indeed, now I know that you all, among whom I have gone preaching the kingdom of God, will see my face no more. Therefore I testify to you this day that I am innocent of the blood of all men. For I have not shunned to declare to you the whole counsel of God. Therefore take heed to yourselves and to all the flock, among which the Holy Spirit has made you overseers, to shepherd the church of God which He purchased with His own blood. For I know this, that after my departure savage wolves will come in among you, not sparing the flock. Also from among yourselves men will rise up, speaking perverse things, to draw away the disciples after themselves. Therefore watch, and

> remember that for three years I did not cease to
> warn everyone night and day with tears.
>
> Ephesians 20:25–31

In the summer of 1998, the head education office transferred me to their largest madrassa of the region, surrounded by a beautiful mountainous landscape west of the coast. Maureena's transfer request to the same town was granted and she started work at the new hospital there. We had returned to the same location where our Middle East journey had begun four years ago, and we were able to lease a palace-like house, making it our home for the next six years.

Before long we realized that this was God's move in our life. He was about to do great things in and through our lives, and with the people of that nation. It didn't take much time to adjust to our new surroundings and get acquainted with people we had lost touch with over the last couple of years.

We embarked upon pursuing a completely different kind of ministry. Our targets were the far-flung, never-reached health and education centers imbedded deep in the mountains where few nonnatives and some local Arab families lived. Within a few days, we contacted some believers stationed at these facilities and let them know we were coming. A church in the United States learned about our endeavor and supplied us with a 4x4 all-terrain vehicle. This made travel on long, rough, dirt, gravel, or desert terrain much easier. We accomplished more than we had anticipated. God was faithful and moving mightily among us.

In order to do outreach at all the specific locations we were targeting, the meetings in these cell groups were held only once a month. God was doing amazing work in the hearts of the people and transforming lives in these locations. People became desperately hungry and passionate for God's presence and His leading.

Many hidden believers in other regions learned through word of mouth that we had started underground churches at different locations throughout our region. They desired to do the same in their location. They contacted Brother Ebenezer and me, inviting us to begin such meetings where they lived too.

Brother Ebenezer and Ambu came down to our place to spend time in prayer and decide whether we should embark upon this challenge or not. After praying and fasting for a couple of days, we came together to share notes both couples had received from the Lord. Both of us were on the same page and the challenge was on. This was not some bungee-jumping, adrenaline-hype game, but a concealed defiance of the law of the land to practice and promulgate an un-Islamic faith. The stakes were high; but so was the joy and divine rewards—nothing would stand as an obstacle to this godly feat.

Our hearts and feet were on fire, and we were ready to embark on a slow but steady national revival. We had not forgotten what God's Word fearlessly articulates: "You are of God, little children, and have overcome them, because He who is in you is greater than he who is in the world" (1 John 4:4). Our hope and strength was only in the great I AM, the One who revealed Himself to be the Lord God of Abraham, Isaac, and Jacob. The Psalmist reiterated this when he said, "I will lift up my eyes to the hills—from whence comes my help? My help comes from the Lord, who made heaven and earth. He will not allow your foot to be moved; He who keeps you will not slumber" (Psalm 121:1–3). What an awesome God we trust in, rely on, and worship.

We had an impossible mission ahead of us; therefore, one weekend Brother Ebenezer, Ambu, Maureena, and I traveled over the mountains to scout the far western area of the land. We felt like the 12 spies that went out to Canaan before taking it. We visited potential believers and families who were interested in starting underground churches in their locations. There were fascinating discussions and we couldn't wait to get feedback from the various people.

It was astounding to see how God was working in the hearts of these men and women. They were being moved by the Holy Spirit to have the audacity to venture out and establish cell groups and underground home churches.

I can just imagine what was going on during the formation of the Acts 2 church and all that followed after the Day of Pentecost. People were thirsting and craving to experience God's presence, which had the dimension to transform anybody that stood in His way. We witnessed again and again the unbelievable manifestation and power of God and knew that He was the same yesterday, today, and forever. We were not satisfied with what we had already experienced, as wonderful as it was. We wanted more.

As we returned from our scouting tour, we were overwhelmed with the doors God had opened for extending His kingdom. We needed people who would be willing to volunteer their time to pursue making this impossible mission fruitful. In the days that followed, God raised many strong men in these locations to stand firm and gear themselves up for the onslaught that was about to take place.

While Brother Ebenezer and Ambu left for the USA to pursue mission studies for a couple of months, we hosted an elderly pastor and his wife from Australia, who had come as tourists to the land. They stayed with us for a while and, after observing our lifestyles, were surprised in the manner we carried out the ministry in these churches. They told us something no one had ever articulated to us before: "If you keep doing ministry like this, you will soon burn out as you seem to be burning the candle from both ends."

We took their advice seriously. So in the future we delegated people to do different jobs, even training some of them for worship and preaching. This helped shed a lot of our responsibilities and gave us needed rest to recuperate from over exhaustion. The downside for this format of management would now make the underground churches vulnerable to wolves in sheep's clothing. We had to be very careful and ever-ready to rightfully identify any attack from the enemy and protect the flock of God. We had to depend more on prayer and trusting the leadership at these locations while leaving everything in God's hands.

The next summer we had the same European couple and some of their friends visit us again. They had returned to the land for prayer walks and to claim it for Christ. We had arranged for some underground renewal meetings while they were with us. These meetings went really well and the church experienced a fresh surge of the Holy Spirit's power in a new dimension. Many in the body were prophesied over and given a word of knowledge or encouragement.

During these meetings, the team surprisingly called my wife and I up to the front and laid hands upon us, prophesying, proclaiming, and imparting the anointing of the Levites upon what was to come in our lives. They said our calling was to be like the Levitical priests, standing in the gap, shepherding God's people, and protecting His flock. The underground church already had a glimpse of it, but now they would bear witness to what was about to happen in the future.

It was amazing to see God's hand work out His plan in a way we had never experienced before. Many were blessed during these meetings and returned to their homes desiring more of Him and less of themselves. Witnessing these series of events in the past few years made the underground church believe with surety that God was about to unleash something incredible in that nation.

The more vigorously the Lord's work advances, the more Satan and his forces get upset at God's people as they become a threat for his kingdom. In the spiritual realm, therefore, that mission becomes chief on

Satan's hit list. One needs to be ready to be attacked by Satan and his forces when involved in the work of the Lord. No matter how long these assaults last, they are inevitable, and one needs to be spiritually and mentally prepared for any kind of occurrence, keeping in mind that they have physical and emotional repercussions. One thing we could not rule out, and that we learned from our experience in ministry, was that the greater a person's calling, the stronger the adversary is against them. This also bore testimony throughout the lives of David and Joseph.

Our family continually pressured us to stop the Lord's work and return back to India. Simultaneously, our worship leader at one of the locations started to rebel as he wanted more power and desired to be known amongst the leadership at the national front of the underground church movement.

At another location we had unwillingly wanted to share the ministry with a person we didn't know at all, but due to distance and time constraints, we allowed him to be a part of our team. A couple of months later, he betrayed us by talking ill to the cell groups in his area about Brother Ebenezer and me. Having no maturity and willingness to check out whether he was telling the truth, these cell groups separated and slowly fizzled out. Apparently, this is what happens when wolves come in wearing sheep's clothing.

We learned through this experience that it was important to test people and know them for some time before inviting them to be a part of our ministry. But through all of this, God was encouraging us—other locations of the underground churches were in full swing. Many lives were being saved for Christ and God was doing great things in our midst.

CHAPTER 9

STEPPING-STONES FOR LAUNCHING

And He said to them, "Go into all the world
and preach the gospel to every creature".

Mark 16:15

We are bound to thank God always for you,
brethren, as it is fitting, because your faith grows
exceedingly, and the love of every one of you
all abounds toward each other, so that we ourselves boast of you among the churches of God
for your patience and faith in all your persecu-
tions and tribulations that you endure, which
is manifest evidence of the righteous judgment
of God, that you may be counted worthy of
the kingdom of God, for which you also suffer;
since it is a righteous thing with God to repay
with tribulation those who trouble you, and to
give you who are troubled rest with us when
the Lord Jesus is revealed from heaven with His
mighty angels, in flaming fire taking vengeance
on those who do not know God, and on those

who do not obey the gospel of our Lord Jesus
Christ.

2 Thessalonians 1:3–8

Work continued to go well at the madrassa where I
taught English as a second language. The morning
would start with the recitation of the Qur'an, and then
class till the afternoon. I had made good friends with
colleagues from different Islamic countries and the local
staff members. I had also gained the love and respect of
many of my students.

During the hours the students were at school, three
times they would participate in Islamic prayers. On one
occasion, a local student did not leave the classroom to
attend these prayers, and so I asked him why he didn't
desire to participate. What surprised me most was that
he was willing to confide to a foreigner what he would
hide from his own community. He said he didn't believe
in what they did and though he looked like a Muslim,
at heart he really wasn't.

He quickly took out his notebook, turned to the last
page, and drew a rough illustration of a cross and quietly
proclaimed to have faith in this alone. This incident left
me in awe, and for months I could not forget about it. I
also understood that there were many secret Christians
living in that country. These men and women looked
like Muslims, but due to the potential threat to their
lives and becoming victims of honor killings, they pro-
fessed and practiced their faith in Christ secretly.

The Qur'an gives instructions for how to deal with nonbelievers of the Islamic faith and presents dire consequences for apostasy:

> Make war on those who have received the Scriptures (Jews and Christians) but do not believe in Allah or in the Last Day. They do not forbid what Allah and His Messenger have forbidden. The Christians and Jews do not follow the religion of truth until they submit and pay the poll tax (jizya), and they are humiliated.
>
> Sura 9:29

> They (kafirs) will be cursed, and wherever they are found, they will be seized and murdered. It was Allah's same practice with those who came before them, and you will find no change in Allah's ways.
>
> Sura 33:60

> They but wish that ye should reject Faith (Islam), as they do, and thus be on the same footing (as they): But take not friends from their ranks until they flee in the way of Allah (from what is forbidden). But if they turn renegades, seize them and slay them wherever ye find them.
>
> Sura 4:89

Christians and Jews are infidels according to the Qur'an; but infidels are also labeled as kafirs (unbelievers). Even though Hindus are polytheists, which means they believe in many gods, they are also kafirs. The terms infidel and polytheist are both religious words, but only kafir shows the common political treatment of Christian, Jew, Hindu, Buddhist, animist, atheist, and humanist; and it should be used instead of unbeliever.

The word unbeliever is a neutral term. The Qur'an defines the kafir as not being neutral. A kafir is not merely someone who does not agree with Islam, but is an evil and disgusting individual, being the lowest form of life. Kafirs can be tortured, killed, lied to, and cheated on. So the usual word unbeliever does not reflect the political reality of Islam.

With no separation of state and faith, and Islam being the predominantly practiced faith in the Middle East, observing the lives of the people drove me to read the Qur'an in order to understand their attitudes, behaviors, psychology, and how they functioned as people in a community. I was then able to better relate to them and answer their questions when they were inquisitive about my faith in Christ.

It seems that Christ is mentioned more times in the Qur'an than the prophet Mohammed. But, according to them, Christ is not divine; He is only considered one of their prophets. To convey the message of salvation through Christ and Him being the God-Man would be a challenge worth taking on. My wife and I chose to unconditionally love these people whom God had created. Our weapon of warfare would be prayer, love, and hospitality.

Maureena kept a Bible in her drawer at work and would not hesitate to read it when alone. On one occasion, a staunch Muslim girl whom she was mentoring asked her what love really was. Maureena asked the girl's permission to share from the Bible, which she reluctantly gave. They shut and locked the office from the inside as Maureena went about ministering to her.

She turned to John 3:16 to share God's love for her and how He acted upon that love by giving His life. Maureena then turned to 1 Corinthians 13 and started to read. By the time Maureena ended that chapter, the Muslim girl was in a pool of tears and in a dilemma as to why the Islamic authorities and mullahs instructed people not to read the Bible. A fire was sparked and she desired to know more.

I befriended many of the Islamic teachers at school; some of them were mullahs in their local communities and managed mosques. I showed them love and cared about them, and we all gathered together during our break time to discuss important family and faith issues. They nicknamed me the Masihi mullah (which means Christian priest).

The regular exchanges that I had with them became the best and most unforgettable conversations I have ever had in my life. On one occasion, we started to discuss Christ on the cross, His death, resurrection, and ascension. They began to refute the biblical narrative and dwelt upon the qur'anic account.

They stated that God had replaced Christ by putting Judas Iscariot on the cross, and Christ was saved and ascended to God. If I hadn't understood the biblical and qur'anic accounts in detailed parallels, I would have floundered. But I stated the biblical narrative and then articulated the qur'anic references to the story. I learned along the way that they stated only one reference from the Qur'an:

> Verily, we have killed the Messiah, Jesus the son of Mary, the apostle of God,... but they did not kill him, and they did not crucify him, but a similitude was made for them. And verily, those who differ about him are in doubt concerning him; they have no knowledge concerning him, but only follow an opinion. They did not kill him, for sure! Nay, God raised him up unto Himself; for God is mighty and wise! And there shall not be one of the people of the Book but shall believe in him before his death; and on the Day of Judgment he shall be a witness against them.
>
> Sura 4:156–157

Since Islam denies Christ's death, it only makes sense they would deny His resurrection also. They therefore deliberately put a veil over the other references, which testified to the death of Christ, His resurrection, and His ascension. Yet there is some hint of this truth in Sura 19:33–34, referencing Jesus: "Peace be upon me the day I was born and the day I die and the day I shall be raised alive. That was Jesus, the son of Mary, and this is the truth of this matter, about which they continue to doubt."

This is as clear as the biblical record, but they just don't know how to grapple with it. The problem was that when I would articulate Sura Maryam to them, our conversation would immediately come to a deadlock and no one knew where to go from there even though I desired the discussion to continue. I always prayed for God to give me the right words to direct the conversation where we all would continue discussing biblical truths in some form or the other. But this did not always happen.

What is even more perplexing and confusing is the Islamic belief that Jesus ascended into Heaven, and that He will die after His second coming, and then will be raised with everyone else in the general resurrection in the end times. When He comes back, He will tell all the Christians to follow Mohammed. This changes the whole New Covenant with Jesus as its focus and His ruling in the kingdom, which is stated in Isaiah 9:6: "For unto us a Child is born, unto us a Son is given; and the government will be upon His shoulder. And His name will be called Wonderful, Counselor, Mighty God, Everlasting Father, Prince of Peace."

Even though people disagreed with us, not once did any of my colleagues, students, or people in my neighborhood, inform the police or authorities about our passionate faith, intent, and evangelistic approach. The secret was to love them like they had never been loved before. We must understand that human beings are the same everywhere we go in the world—people are just hungry for love. And if they saw that we loved them unconditionally, they would overlook everything else and hear what we have to say.

Maureena and I took a short break one day to get away from all the busyness of life, so we could recuperate on an unmanned island in the Arabian Sea. One morning we drove to the nearby beach and hired a fisherman to drop us at the island. He would return in the evening to take us back. As we disembarked on the island, we had a brisk walk around it to determine its inhabitants and we found that we were all alone; if anything was to happen, we were left at God's mercy. There was no cell phone signal available.

So we unpacked our belongings and swam for a while in the ocean; and as the sun rose, the heat got uncomfortable. So we returned to the beach to cook our lunch. After our meal, we shut our eyes and rested under the shade of a bedcover for a while.

As the sun was going down, I returned into the Arabian Sea for a quiet swim when I experienced a stinging sensation in my legs. I had no idea what had happened. The excruciating pain drove me to return to the beach, and I looked behind to see the nemesis of this stealth attack. There, in the crystal clear waters, I saw a bunch of blue jellyfish. I had invaded their space and the result was self-evident.

There was a sudden stutter in my speech, and as their venom kicked in, the feeling of nausea made my head spin turbulently and I felt my body shut down on the soft, white beach. I was unconscious. We had no help or ray of hope—Maureena's voice had a mixture of crying and prayer. We were left at God's mercy.

It took a couple of hours for the toxins in my body to wear out as I regained consciousness and was able to talk normally once again. That evening the fisherman returned to pick us up, and I felt weak but was ready to go back. After arriving on the mainland, I drank a lot of fluids and was almost back to normal. We were now ready to head home.

God was teaching us to depend upon Him completely, no matter what happens in life! Was He preparing us to go to the next level? How we reacted and handled situations like these was important to God. In fact, it was wonderful to be left at God's mercy as we got to witness how good He truly was when we had nothing else to rely on but Him.

The pioneering ministry of planting underground churches in unreached areas still continued. Some places continued to be successful, whereas others did not. We didn't forcefully push or manipulate matters, but allowed the Spirit of God to lead us and establish the work.

One night, as soon as the worship service started at a location close to a naval base, a Buddhist couple from Ceylon entered the home and within few minutes the woman was on the floor foaming at the mouth and screaming obscenities. The worship service continued while Ambu, who has a profound gift of deliverance, started to speak with authority to the demonic spirit in this woman. The fight continued for a couple hours. Though she was freer, she was not completely free.

The next day we went to their home and continued with the deliverance process, which lasted for quite some time before we witnessed complete freedom in this woman. Operating in the gifts of the Holy Spirit, and events like these, played a profound role in establishing and growing the underground churches in the Middle East. These further extended God's kingdom and authenticated the biblical passage that says, "For the kingdom of God is not in word but in power" (1 Corinthians 4:20).

Each of us involved in the ministry had to radically learn to walk and move in the power of the Holy Spirit, being able to be instruments for God's glory. These were just the stepping-stones for steadfastly launching the underground churches in the Middle East.

CHAPTER 10

9/11:
THE INEVITABLE IMPACT

There will be on every high mountain and on every high hill rivers and streams of waters, in the day of the great slaughter, when the towers fall.... Behold, the name of the Lord comes from afar, burning with His anger, and His burden is heavy; His lips are full of indignation, and His tongue like a devouring fire. His breath is like an overflowing stream, which reaches up to the neck, to sift the nations with the sieve of futility; and there shall be a bridle in the jaws of the people, causing them to err.

Isaiah 30:25, 27–28

For He bruises, but He binds up; He wounds, but His hands make whole. He shall deliver you in six troubles, yes, in seven no evil shall touch you. In famine He shall redeem you from death, and in war from the power of the sword. You shall be hidden from the scourge of the tongue, and you shall not be afraid of destruction when it comes.

Job 5:18–21

In the summer of 2001, my younger sister Noor was returning to India with her family after successfully pursuing higher studies in education in the United States for a year. They planned to travel through the Middle East for two weeks before resuming work back home. Arriving at the international airport past midnight in the dead heat, they found their luggage had been lost along the way.

We went home and retrieved the luggage after the airline authorities had located it two days later. They spent a couple of days recuperating from the jet lag and were ready to check out the land. Maureena had taken her annual leave and I was enjoying my paid summer vacation of almost three months. Our mentors were overseas and we were responsible for managing the interior underground ministry.

We took my sister's family for almost all our ministerial tours, and it happened so that we were to cross a part of the Arabian Plateau to minister at some of the underground churches there. After we wound up our last meeting one night, we planned to stay at another location surrounded by the desert. While driving to that location through the jabels,[22] we encountered a deep and broad wadi along the way.

It was pitch dark that night, and we didn't have enough time to see that it was flooded from the torrential rains that had unexpectedly occurred. This was going to be a dangerous feat, and we hoped that God was on our side so that we would not be washed into the sea by the fast currents.

Both my hands firmly gripped the steering wheel as we went through the waters. We could see nothing as the water splashed all over the vehicle, causing it to seem like we were traveling through a swirling tunnel of fast-moving liquid. But we came out on the other side!

We checked for visible traces of damage on the tires and vehicle, but couldn't see any. The vehicle even seemed to run better than before—what just happened could have been fatal if God had not surrounded us with His protection. We could only thank and praise God for His wonderful promise:

> Fear not, for I have redeemed you; I have called you by your name; you are Mine. When you pass through the waters, I will be with you; and through the rivers, they shall not overflow you. When you walk through the fire, you shall not be burned, nor shall the flame scorch you. For I am the Lord your God, the Holy One of Israel, your Savior.
>
> Isaiah 43:1–3

The next few days we visited a number of well-known tourist locations and then returned home safely. This was one of the most overwhelming trips we had ever made.

Before they left, we got into a discussion about the Middle East conflict and the role the West was playing in it. The internal climate within the Middle East was raging hot and they were desperate to bring the West down to their knees. Having lived in the Middle East too long and knowing the people and the land too well, I casually mentioned to my family over dinner that things were so heated up now that it would be inevitable for America to experience an attack from some Muslim fundamentalist group.

I didn't think anything of it because Arab communities conversed openly to one another on this topic and no one was unaware of what it was building up to. It was common knowledge that the attack would come from within and in a subtle manner, but no one really knew when and how it would be executed. As my sister's family had just returned from America, they only talked about how great America was and that it was impossible for anyone to attack it and bring it down. It was time for my sister's family to return to India.

The day of September 11, 2001, went well, and in the evening my wife went to attend the women's Aglow meeting. They had planned to spend time in prayer, worship, and meditating on God's Word.

While she was gone, I wanted to pray and intercede for the people, world situations, and unbelievers I knew. In order to pray for world situations, I usually turned on the television set and turned to CNN to know what was going on, so that I could know what was actually taking place.

It was Tuesday morning in the USA, and people had just started their commute to work. The television screen was filled with unbelievable images of the horrific attack on the World Trade Center, resulting in the Twin Towers toppling to the ground. I immediately called Maureena to let her know what was transpiring in America over the last hour.

On hearing the news, all the women at the meeting got down on their knees and started to intercede for the United States. Unaware to many in the States, believers around the world fervently prayed and interceded for America on a regular basis. The images were flashed on the television not for hours but for the next few days as the situation in the world turned from tranquility to a state of fear and ugliness.

Work the next day was unpleasant as Arab Muslims from all walks of life, no matter where they were from, were excited and continually proclaimed, "At last we have done it. Praise Allah!" This attitude of reprisal sent chills of fear amongst the non-Muslims living in the Middle East. An atmosphere of threatening intimidation and betrayal prevailed amongst the Christians living there.

Wednesday afternoon and evening was spent in dancing processions in the streets, congratulating one another, and distributing goodies. People held posters and banners of Saddam Hussein and Osama Bin Laden, who were hailed as two brave men who stood up against the West in order to protect Islam. Many non-Muslims realized it didn't matter if a person was a liberal or fundamentalist Muslim when it came to stripping the Western countries—they all had the same mindset. Deep down in their hearts they abhorred and were envious of the success of the Western countries.

The hatred they harbored surfaced and was justified by declaring that as long as America bore allegiance to Israel and did not support the Middle Eastern countries in their endeavor to annihilate Israel, then this would continue. One thing was sure: life was now going to get tougher and become more unsafe for non-Muslims, especially for Christians living in the Middle East. One of the most disturbing factors for the non-Muslims was why the so-called self-proclaiming fair Western media failed to broadcast the events of the 9/11 aftermath and its impact in the Middle East while the Qatar based Al-Jazeera news channel continued to do so.

Bin Laden gave a call to all Muslims around the world to unite and destroy the Western infidels and claimed USA for Islam. Whether this was just a nightmare or a long-term agenda would apparently depend upon the Christians and the slumbering church of the West. The more lukewarm it stayed, the more chances it had of being spewed, which would easily usher in Islam to launch their long-anticipated dream. An American retaliation effort with a global coalition was on the table and things on the international front were moving quickly. Henceforth, it was an established fact that the days ahead would not be as smooth as we had witnessed before.

Underground ministry in the Middle East was getting more difficult as there was prevailing suspicion of the West, and anyone who was a Christian was assumed to have some connection with the Western nations.

The primary mindset of an Arab Muslim is that Islam and the functioning of the state go hand in hand—the two cannot be separated. The state cannot function without enforcing Sharia law; there is no segregation between the two because they functionally complement one another. Many Muslims equate secularism with antireligious attitudes; therefore, a state without Sharia law is unfathomable. Any Christian could be easily associated with any of the Western (Christian) countries.

Events since September 11 have dramatically altered the political environment in the Muslim world, a vast and diverse region comprising the band of countries with significant Muslim populations. In the Muslim world, as in others, religion, politics, and culture are intertwined in complicated ways that the West is unable to comprehend. This situation leads to the concept of structural anti-Westernism (or anti-Americanism). This concept holds that Muslim anger has deep roots in the political and social structures of some Muslim countries, and that opposition to certain US policies merely provides the content and opportunity for the expression of this anger.

It differs fundamentally from the type of anti-Americanism that may result from objections to specific US policies in that it is not amenable to amelioration through policy or public diplomacy means. Seemingly, the West is oblivious to their own actions as they pound and intrude into the vital regions of the Arab world. The brunt of the Muslim animosity bears great impact on Arab, Asian, and African Christians residing in the Middle East and Islamic countries.

When I converse with Muslim Arabs, they often connect Christianity to people having wild parties, boozing, womanizing, and peddling drugs. They assume this is what Christianity is made up of and encourages people to have such a lifestyle.

Prodding why they hold this view caused my eyes to open to reality. Most of the television channels are free to air on Arab soil, and with the satellite dish culture invading almost every Arab family, they have access to every conceivable channel. So the media and the over accessibility of these channels assist them in forming a common Arab view.

Muslim Arabs perceive that the West is double faceted, as on some channels you will hear televangelists preaching from the Bible, and then the same channel will be later dedicated to pornography. They are not able to comprehend as to how someone could be preaching from the Bible at one moment, and then the next thing on is pornography. This has set a bad example and continues to do so without any form of integrity. We cannot defend anything here because as Christians, even though we talk the walk, we are unable to walk the talk. We need to get our act together, set our lives right, and begin to exemplify Christ not only in our talk but, more significantly, in our walk.

Many of us have thought considerably about the events of 9/11 and their resulting aftermath. It is evident the West inclines to have an opinion contradicting the insightful observation of Christians living in the Middle East. I will not hesitate to share it here, so that if any of the readers are thinking otherwise, they will desire God to open their eyes, ears, and hearts to comprehend the message He is trying to give to Christians living in the West. It is time that we wake up from our slumber and giftedly discern what God is trying to convey to each one of us in the body of Christ. This is not a time to cover our sins and choose to continue on that perishable path so we don't spark similar events in the future.

Amongst Middle Eastern Christians, it is common knowledge that 9/11 was God's judgment on America. Pastors like the late David Wilkerson reiterated the same thoughts, but they were the extreme minority. Most preachers in America were trying to deny that God would have anything to do with those horrific events.

God has always talked to His people through symbolism (Daniel, Ezekiel, and Revelation are packed with it). Most of us were able to perceive the symbolism of this event: the World Trade Center clearly symbolized the wealth of the world, but America's wealth in particular. It was a clear warning that God would judge the United States through economic disaster. And the Pentagon symbolized America's military, being a sign that He will judge them by weakening them against their enemies, which seemed clear and already underway.

The September 11 attack was a big event in that it was that the US been attacked on their own land; but it was a small event compared to what it could have been. It was clearly a warning from God, saying, "Repent or there will be more to come." We have forgotten that if God is a God of love, He is also a God of wrath and judgment. If these aspects of God's character are omitted with the advent of the New Testament, then the future final judgment doesn't hold any truth.

The biblical trend has always been that when God's nation (Israel in the past) sinned, turned their face against God, and continued to walk in an ungodly lifestyle, God allowed their enemies to prevail over them with the intention that they would hear God's message loud and clear and adhere to His ways and live in obedience.[23] Israel's reaction in circumstances like these is recorded in the Bible, and yet we in America fail to see that and we walk the same path. Just like Israel, we have not learned from the blunders we have made in the past and continue to tread recklessly.

Did America repent after these attacks? Not really, at least in the long run. Out of fear for their own lives, the churches in America for the next few weeks were packed with attendees who had not visited them for ages. We sang loud choruses of "God Bless America," effectively denying that we had anything to repent of or that God was trying to speak to us. As the hangover of the 9/11 attacks faded, so did most of the new attendees at churches around the nation.

What happens when a nation ignores God's warnings of judgment? Judgment keeps coming. America has not repented and today is clearly looking far worse than what it was when it's forefathers established this nation on Judeo-Christian foundations.

The West is oblivious of the fact that the echo of the 9/11 attacks was heard by Christians living in persecuted nations overseas. The body of Christ outside the United States was clear on this matter as well, but confusion still prevailed in the homeland. And we should not forget that "God is not the author of confusion but of peace" (1 Corinthians 14:33).

In the last few years, God has given us the opportunity to witness a great and mighty awakening, renewal, revival, and astounding growth in the body of Christ in persecuted lands. Instantaneously, the downward spiral of the church in the USA has been taking place. If this is the state of affairs when approximately 95 percent of the world's pastors live in America, what will happen if there are just a handful left?

The events of 9/11 have had an inevitable impact upon the entire world, but upon the United States in particular. What America needs is God's fire to visit them again, restoring passion and desire for Him and His ways.

CHAPTER 11

FRESHFIRE

"Is not My word like a fire?" says the Lord, "and like a hammer that breaks the rock in pieces?".

Jeremiah 23:29

John answered, saying to all, "I indeed baptize you with water; but One mightier than I is coming, whose sandal strap I am not worthy to loose. He will baptize you with the Holy Spirit and fire".

Luke 3:16

God designed the human soul to be passionate and committed to Him. This is the only way humanity can function at its fullest. Without abandonment to God, our hearts sink into restlessness, boredom, and frustration. There must be something in our lives that is worth risking everything for. God intended our souls to be fascinated with Jesus. Our highest development and greatest fulfillment lie in worshiping and serving Jesus with all our hearts, souls, minds, and strength.

Through the past ten years of ministry we have had several setbacks, but God worked all those things together for our good and His glory. Even though we could not see it with our physical eyes, we could sense the profound shifts in the spiritual realm that were taking place. God was setting the stage for grander things to come—we were only unaware of how and where they would be manifested. But that should never be our concern as that is the work of God, and we should simply focus on doing our part.

I was invited to preach in an underground home church at a town that was once the demonic headquarters of the ancient world. Whenever I drove through the town, I would encounter an uncontrollable forward thrust on my vehicle at a specific crossroads at the periphery of town. It took me by surprise when I experienced it for the first time.

I asked some of the nonlocals living in that area about my experience, and they had no idea about the reason for such encounters. So I approached some of the natives and asked them about the situation. Since we were strangers and foreigners, they initially showed reluctance to answer any of my questions. But my inquisitive eagerness and humility gradually gained their trust and made them spill the beans.

They explained to us, "Once upon a time, this town happened to be the demonic capital of the ancient world, and the location that you drive your vehicle through was the exact place where the kings of nearby kingdoms would congregate to have important meetings. Therefore, when driving through that location you feel like you are driving through a wall, sensing a jolting forward. You are apparently barging through their meeting, and they don't like it. In the spiritual realm, they are just throwing you off and that is why you experience the jolt."

As our travels became more frequent through that area, we would mentally and physically prepare ourselves to accept and endure that jolt as we came closer to the location. And we eventually got used to it since we traveled through the town nearly every weekend.

One Friday afternoon, Brother Ebenezer, Ambu, Maureena, and I showed up at a meeting in this same town. The house was already overflowing with people as they rubbed shoulders with one another in a tight room. At the same time, the afternoon azaan[24] could be heard at a distance, followed by prayers and a sermon that went on at a local mosque.

Our meeting started with exuberant worship. Many raised their hands, fell on their knees and faces, and sang joyously to the Lord. We witnessed many women crying out and weeping to God. It seemed that the body of Christ was one in the Spirit and were in complete surrender to the Lord.

After the sermon, there was more worship in order for people to respond to God's message. As I stood behind the podium, I experienced a physical trembling and thought I was going to topple over. Quietly, I stepped down and summoned Brother Ebenezer to preside over the meeting. He seemed to experience the same exact thing, so he came back to stand in the pews. God had surely showed up and presided over the meeting. The Holy Spirit overwhelmed me and gave me prophetic words for many, revealing the ailments of different people and assuring them of complete healing and recovery.

A month later, when I returned to the same location, I heard the testimonies of the prophetic words and physical healings that had taken place. I had never experienced or used these spiritual gifts before in my life. My mentor tapped into and discerned what these gifts were in my life, but it was my choice to operate in them by faith. One wrong assessment or discernment could have cost us all our ministerial endeavors. The cost was very high, but we had to attentively listen to the Holy Spirit so that God would be glorified in all that we were doing.

On hearing of the events that had transpired in that city, many other towns started to invite us to begin meetings in their towns as well. God led us to a larger town north of the demonic capital.

After just a couple of meetings in that town, we experienced the obliteration of the demonic clouds prevailing upon the lives of the people. God was faithful and many people were blessed as they had unbelievable breakthroughs in their lives; many who had struggles and strongholds were set completely free. A number of people who had physical infirmities were healed as well. In all of this we witnessed God being glorified and exalted. It was all about Him, and He would not share His glory with any man.

After having a wonderful and powerful night at another one of the underground churches, we returned home to sleep before going to work early the next morning. At 3 a.m. I received a phone call from

Brother Ebenezer telling me that a couple from our congregation had been in a car accident that night and we needed to care for them. So we made some calls to find out where the accident had been, what had really happened, and where they were now located. My wife and I arrived at the hospital just before daybreak and proceeded directly to the intensive care unit.

From his head to his toes, Madhav had multiple fractures and was strapped to a bed. His wife, Madhu, had a couple of bruises and was in the women's ward; while his young daughter only had a fractured shoulder and a couple of bruises. His son, who sat in the passenger's seat during the crash, had flown out of the car's windshield, hit his head on an electric pole, and died instantly. I inquired from some of the medical technicians and nurses about what this family had undergone and the care they were getting. I also got to know their story through one of their friends who had immediately arrived upon hearing of their accident.

He told me about how the family had booked their airline tickets to fly to their homeland for vacation, and were returning from the capital late at night after making some last minute gift purchases for family and friends. As they neared our town, while Madhav was driving, he was tired and could not keep his eyes open, and just dozed off for a few seconds. Thus, his vehicle veered off the road and hit a telephone pole. The impact brought about injuries to the family, death to their 7-year-old son, and totaled their car. Madhav blacked out during the impact and only regained consciousness after being brought to the emergency room. He did not know the whereabouts of his family, and neither was he aware of the news of the death of his son.

The man went on to tell me, "Out of fear, none of us here are able to tell him about the crash and the death of his son. Can you do it, please?" He challenged me to tell Madhav about what had happened, and about the death of his son. I had no idea how to go about it, so I went into silent prayer, asking God to give me the strength and the right words to state the facts correctly and without any offense.

As the news got out, I observed many of Madhav's friends and well-wishers trickling in to visit him. I came to him and inquired about his well-being. Madhav answered with nods, and with simultaneous eye and facial expressions, trying to communicate incomprehensible information. The medical attendees told him to rest and refrain from exerting himself while talking. After a while, his wife and daughter were also brought in to see him, and he again expressed himself through facial expressions and body language.

We didn't really know how the last two hours had passed. I requested for all of Madhav's visitors to surround him while holding hands and we spent time praying. As I started to pray, it was audible to all those around. Though it was a long prayer, I remember some specific utterances:

> We don't know why this had to happen, but we know that You have some beautiful purpose in it. Just as You gave and took away from Job, and yet he worshiped and gave You thanks, we would like to follow suit—You gave Mani to

Madhav and Madhu and took him away for a purpose that You alone know, and we are no one to question You. We submit to Your understanding and believe that You know things will get better for us.

I pray that You would please give Madhav and Madhu's family strength and endurance to go through this hard trial. And now we want to praise and worship You and give You thanks even in this circumstance, for that is the will of God in Christ Jesus our Lord. We ask this all in the name of our Lord and Savior, Jesus Christ. Amen.

After the prayer, Madhav called me over to talk. He was thankful that I had made him aware of the news of his son's death; and right there and then he prayed a prayer of brokenness and then praised and thanked God for the death of his only son. What a testimony to God and a witness to Madhav's friends and people in that hospital!

All of us left for our jobs and made occasional visits to the hospital till Madhav and his family returned back to their home. The hard part was yet to come—the funeral of their son, Mani, that weekend. Due to his immobility, Madhav was not able to attend his son's funeral.

The funeral site was packed with people. As Brother Ebenezer Vijay presided over the event, everyone was overwhelmed watching the funeral procession and ceremony take place. Women wailed and cried as the coffin was lowered into the bosom of the earth. Finally, the men covered it with soil and allowed people to lay flowers and wreaths at the site. Many believers from all over the region had come to witness this solemn event.

Even though it was a daytime event in the scorching heat, everything went well, and many were blessed to be there. Even in this horrific circumstance, God was faithful and good to all of us involved. We could see His hand in the events that had transpired as He had steadily steered the spirit of Madhav to become passionate about Him and be completely sold out to serve Him. Madhav's call and walk with God had begun.

Though we still faced persecution and horrific circumstances, God was still good and working everything out for our good and the growth of His kingdom. Paul's words to the Romans were really true: "And we know that all things work together for good to those who love God, to those who are the called according to His purpose" (Romans 8:28).

CHAPTER 12

LEARNING THROUGH ADVERSITIES

For the kingdom of God is not in word but in power.

1 Corinthians 4:20

For God has not given us a spirit of fear, but of power and of love and of a sound mind.

2 Timothy 1:7

The ministry in the northwestern towns was picking up gradually, and people were responding positively. The underground meetings were exhilarating, and the congregants were being challenged to allow the Holy Spirit to transform them and become passionate for Christ.

We occasionally used to take the northern highway during the day to drive and minister to people along the way, and return late at night while driving on the dirt roads through the dark desert and Arabian jabels. On one occasion, in order to save time, we traveled during the day on the dirt road and encountered heavy rains and flash floods in the wadis.

As the sky was overcast and it grew dark, we encountered a thunderstorm and then a heavy downpour. We had completed more than half of our journey into the rugged jabels when we realized that we would be hit by flash floods along the way. Going back was not an option at this point as the wadis we had crossed would be completely flooded by now.

We had no other choice but to continue forward. In circumstances like these, there was always the danger of being washed into the sea. Because of this, Maureena started to pray for safety and for the rains to slow down, reminding me of James 5:17–18:

> Elijah was a man with a nature like ours, and he prayed earnestly that it would not rain; and it did not rain on the land for three years and six months. And he prayed again, and the heaven gave rain, and the earth produced its fruit.

If Elijah was like us, as the Bible declares, then surely we could also fervently pray and ask God to meet the desire of our hearts. After all, we were not asking for some casual entertainment, but for His kingdom work. It was apparent that God was showing us that He is a God who answers us when we call upon Him.

The rainwaters rolled down the wadis ferociously, and it was a scary sight to see the flash flood approaching. It would hit us within just a few minutes. As soon as it hit our vehicle, however, we felt a slight jolt as the current picked up, but nothing significant happened. It was more or less like a soft wave hitting us on the seashore, and then we gradually saw the storm and rains die out. What was going on?

It seemed as though these climatic conditions were going to be this way for the long haul, but suddenly the water was now receding! The only explanation of this was that God was answering our prayers! So we picked up speed, cruised through the running waters, and reached our destination safely.

That night, most of the congregants attending the meeting could never have imagined that we would make it. It was a major surprise for them when we walked through the doors, safe and sound. By us being there, God was demonstrating His faithfulness and immense love for the people.

The meetings in the northwestern towns were picking up fast as people flocked in numbers that packed the venues. God was doing unbelievable things in their lives. Most of them testified of being reborn and transformed by the conviction of the Holy Spirit. The demands of the congregants grew and they desired us to be present at these meetings every week.

Our frequent travels took us through the wadi routes, which also had major consequences. When we traveled through the jabels, our vehicle recurrently got flat tires. I usually kept two spares with us to suffice for any inconvenient event, as many times I would change the flats during the afternoons when the heat was over 120 degrees. There were actually a number of times I had burnt my back and hands while doing it.

There were also numerous times I changed the flats in the middle of the night, not really knowing and caring about the possible presence of dangerous animals, scorpions, snakes, or hostile tribes. Maureena would faithfully keep me encouraged so that I would not lose hope. Besides Brother Ebenezer and Ambu, Maureena was the earthly source of my strength and reassurance throughout this time.

These episodes caused me to return to God's Word again and again as a wonderful reminder of His faithfulness and goodness toward us. I continually read David's words from Psalm 23:

> Yea, though I walk through the valley of the shadow of death, I will fear no evil; for You are with me; Your rod and Your staff, they comfort me. You prepare a table before me in the presence of my enemies; You anoint my head with oil; my cup runs over. Surely goodness and mercy shall follow me all the days of my life.
>
> Psalm 23:4–6

Due to the frequency of the flat tires, I got the vehicle checked by a tire mechanic who told me that the tires were not good quality and unsuitable for mountainous terrain. So I bought new tires, and changed all of them so that we could endure the rugged terrain. The change worked well and the frequency of flats reduced incredibly. Through all these events, God taught us to depend on Him completely and not worry about worldly fears, but to fear Him above everything else.

During cooler temperatures, Maureena and I would occasionally go into the Arabian jabels seeking solitude to meditate on God's Word, His promises, and worship Him with psalms and hymns. At the same time, this would also give us an opportunity to spend time together in prayer, seeking God's guidance for direction in ministry and for our lives.

God was always faithful in this endeavor as He gave us direction and focus to our ministry. He continued to reveal prophetically important issues related to the congregants and about the future. This helped us associate with the experiences of Moses as he went to Mount Sinai to meet God on behalf of the Israelites. These experiences overwhelmed and triggered an unarticulated longing for God deep within us, giving us a greater desire for His presence. Needless to say, the visits to the jabels were with great eagerness and anticipation.

We arranged for one night each month to have night vigils at our home. We did this with the understanding of not wanting to have many vehicles parked outside, as this would perk up the eyes and ears of the neighbors and draw undue attention to us. So I would pick up people around 9 in the evening after the neighborhood went to sleep, and the vigil began around 10 p.m. Our living room, which was more of a hall, would be completely packed with people who would congregate to worship God exuberantly and expect great things from Him.

We would praise and worship God, read psalms, pray, and fellowship during this time. This wouldn't be in any particular order, but we would go through cycles of this late into the night, carrying over even into the early morning hours. The gifts of the Holy Spirit would be profoundly operative. Many would receive prophetic words, words of knowledge, discernment, and healings would flow from God's throne of grace. One could sense the venue being saturated with an incomprehensible presence of God.

Though the experience was overwhelmingly profound, no one was ready or satisfied to leave at daybreak. None showed signs of being tired but all of us were overflowing with spiritual energy—we were hungry for more of God, more of His presence and less of ourselves.

One day Brother Ebenezer realized he was being followed by secret police in plain clothes and unmarked vehicles. All his activities were being documented. He didn't know how long they had been following him, but he believed it was not a daily affair but only happened occasionally. This was discouraging to all of us, but it didn't keep us from doing what we had to do. To thwart this activity, Brother Ebenezer and I would frequently exchange vehicles, thus confusing the stalkers.

Though there was a possibility of a second Gulf War brewing in the region, all our hearts were at peace as we knew that these were just beads in the thread that would lead to larger events in the future, fulfilling biblical prophecy. Despite numerous setbacks, the ups and downs in the lives of the people and ministry, the believers had become daring to desire God and be passionate for His presence. There was a fresh fire raging in the hearts of the people of God, and they were ready to go to any extent to contain it.

CHAPTER 13

SECOND GULF WAR

"Please inquire of the Lord for us, for Nebuchadnezzar king of Babylon makes war against us. Perhaps the Lord will deal with us according to all His wonderful works that the king may go away from us." Then Jeremiah said to them,..."Thus says the Lord God of Israel: 'Behold, I will turn back the weapons of war that are in your hands, with which you fight against the king of Babylon and the Chaldeans who besiege you outside the walls; and I will assemble them in the midst of this city'".

Jeremiah 21:2–4

And you will hear of wars and rumors of wars. See that you are not troubled; for all these things must come to pass, but the end is not yet.

Matthew 24:6

The ties between Israel and the contemporary body of Christ are counterparts that cannot be detached. Their relationship is like the nail and the finger. Therefore, the demise of Israel would easily usher in the death of Christ's church in the West. Most people who understand and comprehend this parallel are not able to articulate it rightfully, because what ultimately happens to Israel (physical) will bear profound significance on the fate of the church (spiritual). This ordeal is more spiritual than physical!

The bearing of the second Gulf War was giving room to the empires in the Middle East to change some on their laws, especially those targeted toward the immigrants. The noose on their private activities would yet become tighter. If one had keen eyes, they could see a greater influx of secret police in plain clothes hanging about in public with their ears perked up to the conversations floating around.

One had to be careful in their public discussions, as the freedom of speech doesn't really exist in such countries. Even during our underground meetings, we had to stay quiet for fear of being heard. A slight audible elevation of praise, worship, or preaching could easily bring the big bees to the hive. Because of this, the congregants had to be very discrete in their expressions and speech during the worship service.

As soon as the Gulf War began, the demesne decided to halt the entry of all non-Islamic literature, software, movies, or music in the nation. Not only were Bibles and other such materials banned, but Our Daily Bread was also banned. We used to take risks every three months to smuggle and Xerox hundreds of copies to distribute all over the land.

During the course of the years, ODB had become a powerful devotional tool for many believers in the Middle East, always bringing encouragement to believers and unbelievers alike. When new converts showed interest in getting baptized, we would privately take them to the wadis and baptize them in the streams of the desert. These scenarios always reminded me of John the Baptist baptizing Jesus in the Jordan River, which just happens to flow through the northern part of the Arabian Desert.

A young lady by the name of Kavita, who just got married a couple of years ago, had left her husband in her home country and started to teach English at a madrassa in our town. At times, when she was lonely, she would seek human company to fill that void. It was some of her colleagues that introduced her to our meetings. Though she was not a practicing Christian, she had some vague knowledge of attending church in her childhood.

During these meetings, her soul was passionately ignited for God, and she expressed a desire to be baptized. I took up this matter with Brother Ebenezer, and so one Friday morning we baptized her near the copper fields. She continued to be a faithful follower of Christ and attend our meetings regularly. That year, after returning from her summer vacation, she wanted to meet with us to discuss an important matter. My wife and I listened to her short but bitter story.

She told us that though she had been married for a couple of years, her husband had not taken interest in their sexual life. She always had a hunch that he was either involved with someone else or had some sexual problems. During summer vacation, however, she found out that he was sexually involved with another man, which broke her heart—she didn't know how to deal with it. But since she arrived home from her holiday, she became involved with someone else she had met. So she asked, "Should I divorce my husband and get married to this gentleman?"

We were shocked, not really knowing how to answer her, but consoled her to the point where she felt satisfied, however. I took up this matter with Brother Ebenezer, who spent some time talking with and advising Kavita. In the due course of that year, we learned that she had divorced her husband and married the gentleman she had introduced to us. Such events in the lives of the people we knew always broke our heart. We could do nothing but rely on God to heal them.

Through the process of time and relentless passion, our night travels to faraway health centers and public schools in the jabels and wadis, where paved roads did not exist, got more intense. We would target certain believers living in those vicinities and encourage them to hold nightly meetings once in a while to accommodate all those living in nearby areas. On such occasions there would always be some hungry non-Christians seeking to know and find the truth.

At one instance, there was a Hindu lady attending one of our monthly meetings. Some of her female colleagues made her aware of such gatherings, and she expressed some interest in knowing about Christ. They even gave her a copy of the Bible and the "JESUS" movie.

After one of our meetings, she came forward as she had made a choice to accept Christ as her Savior and

Lord. Subsequently, the believers living close to her would continually encourage her in her daily walk and growth in Christ. As Maureena and I lived at a distance, we could only support and know about her welfare during our visits, but we could not thank God enough for an outstanding support system He had given us there.

Even during the war, our visits to the targeted places in the wadis and jabels did not fail. As we would arrive at these locations, many times God would keep my spiritual eyes open and allow me to see beyond the physical realm: I would be able to witness demonic forms and images dancing and hollering on the mountain tops. This was God's warning and indication to me that there was a profound presence and influence of demons residing in that area. We just had to be spiritually prepared and equipped to stand against and break down the strongholds in that vicinity.

These kinds of encounters always made it important for us to gear up for any awkward event, even though we never desired them. We spent a lot of time in prayer and fasting to counteract and diffuse any demonic activity we would encounter. We spent time prayer walking in and around these vicinities, and even quelled demonic interference and possessions when we encountered such people in our meetings.

The Gulf War being waged in the physical realm had greater parallels and implications in the spiritual warfare we daily encountered in our underground ministry. The war was not of flesh and blood, and the target was never people but the unseen powers in the spiritual realm that ruled the domain and mesmerized the hearts and minds of the people. It was a hard task, but not inevitable because we belonged to a God of all impossibilities.

I remember that when the disciples came to Jesus after being unable to do miracles or drive out demonic spirits, they asked why this was so. Matthew writes,

> Then the disciples came to Jesus privately and said, "Why could we not cast it out?"
>
> So Jesus said to them, "Because of your unbelief; for assuredly, I say to you, if you have faith as a mustard seed, you will say to this mountain, 'Move from here to there,' and it will move; and nothing will be impossible for you. However, this kind does not go out except by prayer and fasting."
>
> Matthew 17:19–21

During the course of our walk with Christ over the past many years, we had dwelt on and learned this covert mystery that Jesus had disclosed to His disciples. And now it was coming in handy quite frequently.

On many occasions, when we returned late at night from the meetings in a pitch dark surrounding in the mountainous regions, it was not only dangerous and fearful but nerve-racking. We had to drive over rocks, boulders, pits, gravel, sand, and wade through streams.

When Maureena was busy at work, I would sometimes go and return by myself. Anything could happen on these trips: we could encounter hostile tribes, poisonous snakes, and scorpions; we could bump into the secret police; we could encounter rain, storms, and flash floods; and the lights or the vehicle itself could even stop working. We were always left at God's mercy and believed He was watching over us, which was the best place to be.

We always made it a point to stay in an atmosphere of prayer, worship, and listening to God's Word on tape as we were driving. God gave us immense strength, wisdom, and encouragement to carry out His work during this time. These events always reminded me what the prophet Zechariah said, "This is the word of the Lord: 'Not by might nor by power, but by My Spirit,' says the Lord of hosts" (Zechariah 4:6). We know that we could have never done these feats in our own strength and can rightfully acknowledge that this was the power and the Spirit of God within us.

We had a number of friends working at the naval and air bases who would share stories of what was really going on during the second Gulf War. As the monarchy was an ally of the West, some islands which they owned were given as a base to America to house their aircrafts, heavy artillery machinery, and soldiers. Sometimes we would get opportunities to meet and talk to American soldiers when they would come on the mainland for shopping and entertainment.

Even one of the heavily fortified and guarded secret runways and helipads were built in the wilderness adjacent to our town. During late nights we could hear sorties landing and taking off. Our friends working at the air base in the capital told us about mysterious aircrafts, which they had never seen in their lifetime, landing at supersonic speeds, refueling, and taking off again in a flash, all under the cover of darkness. Everyone was banned from going near or being in close proximity of these planes. Something was going on that they didn't want anyone in the world to be aware of; they were also protecting the military from any internal or external infiltrations.

I'm sure everyone knew that this war was more high-tech and computer aided, and was focused on precisely marked targets. This was giving us ideas as well in the realm of the Spirit. When we minister to people, we should not randomly just go out there to minister, but we should precisely mark out the people we are going to target for Christ and then pursue them without any hesitation. The Lord will be by our side no matter what!

At the madrassa, a close Muslim colleague, Salem, whom I used to have faith discussions with, one day asked me, "Hey, Ustad Ajai, please get me the Ingeel[25] and the 'Yeshua' movie you talked about."

I responded, "Sure, my brother. Tomorrow you shall have them. Farewell! May God bless you." I was really happy to part with some more of the evangelism tools as long as someone was being reached and drawn to Christ.

The next day I brought the two items and left them in my car, thinking I would give them to Salem during break or after school was let out. I approached him during the break and asked him when I could give him the items. This would be similar to buying or selling drugs in the United States—if caught red-handed, I could easily go to jail for a long time. The stakes were high but well worth it.

Salem took me aside and said, "Yesterday, when I went home, I called my mullah and talked to him about receiving these items from you. He told me that it was completely prohibited in Islam; therefore, I will not be taking them from you. I am sorry, Ustad Ajai, but I have to be obedient to my mullah and adhere to the Islamic teachings."

I responded, "The choice is still yours—I can get them to you whenever you desire or change your mind; but remember, you might never get such a golden opportunity in your life to know and get acquainted with the prophet Isaa Masihi again." He simply shrugged his shoulders as he left disappointed and dismayed.

The Islamic faith does not allow its followers to have access to other religious material so that they're not confused with all the different religions available, and so they're not influenced by these faiths and become renegades. This would be a rebellion in Islam and could cause others to experiment in the same way, leading them to ultimately deny their faith. So in order to protect their religion from the influence of other faiths, Islam has devised and taken a strong stand against receiving or reading any other religious materials.

They want every Muslim to adhere to and abide by the Islamic and qur'anic teachings. They cannot even stand passive intimidation from any faith. I believe this will be detrimental to their global survival and sustenance. Through my encounter with Salem, one could see spiritual warfare being played out explicitly. What can we do in such circumstances?

We should not ever fear Muslims, for they are just like you and me. Rather, we should pray for their souls, love them as they have never been loved before, without any conditions, and pursue them genuinely, opening our lives to them so that they can trust and confide in us. This can radically win their hearts and souls for Jesus Christ.

We must never forget that it is not about Islam, neither is it about us; but it is all about Christ the King! The question we need to ask is, Do we live as Yeshua's ambassadors by displaying the fruit of the Holy Spirit, exemplifying Him through our lives? This is the only thing that will impact and influence the Muslims on their turf.

The underlying imagery of the Gulf Wars was an evident implication for the spiritual warfare that has already been waging there for decades. The significance is not in winning, losing, or coming to a draw in the war. The significance is in endearing the Middle East for Christ!

CHAPTER 14

REVIVEDPASSION

Who makes His angels spirits, His ministers a
flame of fire.

Psalm 104:4

They were all with one accord in one place. And
suddenly there came a sound from heaven, as of
a rushing mighty wind, and it filled the whole
house where they were sitting. Then there
appeared to them divided tongues, as of fire,
and one sat upon each of them. And they were
all filled with the Holy Spirit.

Acts 2:1–4

Oh, the sense of anticipation that filled my heart as
I realized that the Lord had affirmation and affection
for me. I was now confident before Him. It seemed
as though it was too good to be true! I wept for joy.
And when the tears finally ceased, I could sense the
anger, bitterness, guilt, and condemnation beginning
to diminish in my heart. My little, flickering flame
of human zeal was replaced by a blaze of passionate
love for a glorious person. His intense devotion and

ardent affection for me far exceeded that of my earthly father's—I realized I would never be the same again.

To return from where we began would be impossible as Maureena and I had tasted the best of the Lord and desired more of Him and less of us. God was not only reviving us from the inside out, but also a spark swept like a forest fire in the hearts of all those who stood in its path. God showed up at our meetings and did great wonders and miracles in the lives of His people; the profound manifest power of God was poured out in these meetings. It was an overwhelming joy to witness something which is still a taboo and unheard of in the Middle East.

At one of our locations, I encountered an Iraqi Muslim doctor who was invited to attend our meetings. He entered the place while we worshiped on our knees with hands lifted high and without any hesitation; he emulated what we did and listened patiently to the Word of God.

After our meeting, I greeted him and spent some time talking with him. I learned that his life was tipping back and forth. Grievingly, he told me, "Brother, I'm the youngest of five brothers and sisters in my family. Because the ones older than me aren't married, I can't be—but I desire to be married."

In this part of the world, the familial and cultural impacts are greater than one's faith, not to mention a sensitive issue too, so I had to tread very carefully here. I asked him, "What is really holding you back from marriage?"

"We don't find girls anymore in Iraq," he said.

I asked, "Why so?"

"It seems like the war with Iran took most of them away," he replied. "And now with the American invasion, whatever is left will also disappear into thin air. I just feel devastated. I don't know what to do!"

"There are girls from other countries you could potentially think about," I told him.

He retorted by saying, "That is not an option, as we are a very traditional and conservative family, and it would be completely unacceptable amongst my kinsfolk. In fact, when we give our sisters and daughters for marriage in our community, only then will we also receive."

He started to weep and this gave me an opportunity to lovingly console him and introduce Christ softly. I said, "With God there is nothing impossible. If He desires so, He can raise up Iraqi girls right here. We must submit and be obedient to His will in our lives."

The believers promised me that they would continually keep a close watch on him and assist him through this quandary. You never know, he might just come around for Christ. Though he accepted the Bible we gave him, we were greatly troubled in our hearts for his predicament and wanted to be a source of strength and help to him. But what could we do?

Before leaving that night, I put my hands around his shoulders, hugged him, and prayed for him. As we left the location, we were reflecting upon Abram, Sarai, and Lot who were born and raised in Ur (Iraq) before God intruded in their lives and called them to Canaan

(Promised Land). Couldn't He do it with this physician as well?

As usual, Ramadan came, when the entire Islamic world would fast and pray from sunup to sundown for 29–30 days.[26] Fasting during Ramadan was mandatory for every adult living in the country. I once witnessed a European couple having a sandwich at a bus stop during Ramadan when a police car pulled in and whisked them off to prison to be released only after the month of Ramadan was over.

Brother Ebenezer and I devised a regular annual protocol of starting our fast five days before Ramadan and ending it five days after, thus taking the challenge to fast for the entire 40 days at one stretch. During this time, our working hours were reduced so it became easier to carry out the fast. We spent time in personal prayer, worship, and meditating on God's Word. Above everything, we prayed for the Islamic world to come to Christ and that God would appear in dreams and visions to those who were walled in and unreachable.

We also delved into spiritual warfare by counteracting all the demonic spells and qur'anic proclamations over the land. During late evenings, we would take prayer walks in different towns, surround the targeted mosques, and pray fervently for the strongholds to melt. It was during fasting and prayer that we experienced the unprecedented power of the Holy Spirit and an easy flow, manifestation, and operation of His gifts. I didn't understand how this worked, but it worked profoundly well.

Our faithfulness, loyalty, and disciplined lifestyle played a vital role in God doing His work through our lives. Jesus disclosed to His disciples that the secret of moving in the power of the Holy Spirit was a lifestyle of continual fasting and prayer. We were now experiencing this power on a daily basis.

Every year, the days of Ramadan were exciting and there would be a complete revamping of the national climate. The day would more or less be a solemn drag with lethargy and nothing much done, but after sundown people would have fun, eating, drinking, and playing soccer and volleyball late into the night.

One evening, as the sun went down and people were breaking their fast, we drove deep into the rugged jabels on the dirt road and halted only after arriving at our destination—a lonely accommodation on the outskirts of the village. A small group of believers (girls) were going to meet in the bedroom of a seeker, and they had also invited a Muslim girl whom they had been ministering to for a couple of weeks.

As we opened with worship, everyone there sensed and testified to a powerful move of God, bearing witness to His Word: "But thou art holy, O thou that inhabitest the praises of Israel" (Psalm 22:3 KJV). I preached from God's Word for about an hour, and then we responded through praise and worship. Tears flowed in that room and we could see that these women were passionately in love with their Creator.

The Spirit of God prompted me to move in the prophetic realm and pronounce that God was going to do mighty deeds that night with the women. I proclaimed that a girl in that room, who had irregular menstrual bleeding and writhed in pain throughout her life, was going to be healed that night.

Upon hearing this, a Muslim girl got up and announced, "I am ready to accept Christ as my Savior and follow Him all the days of my life." We were all shocked and helped her to pray the prayer of repentance, adopting her into the body of Christ. This was an answer not only to our prayers but also a great victory in spiritual warfare as we had fasted and prayed for Muslims to come to Christ.[27] This could jeopardize future missions, putting everyone's life in that room on the line; and if this girl informed her family, she would be putting herself at great risk.

Under Sharia law, a Muslim who converts to Christianity has essentially signed his or her own death warrant. The penalty for conversion is death, which could possibly take the shape of an honor killing. God had showed up and done a wonderful thing. We didn't know what the future looked like, but we didn't really need to know. We knew that if we trusted that God was with us, then who could stand against us?

After that meeting, a young lady came to my wife and disclosed that she was the one who had the menstrual imbalance. Whenever we met her after that, she testified to the fact that she was completely healed. As we returned home that night, with only the headlights of our vehicle being visible amidst the pitch darkness of the wadis and jabels, we knew that God was well pleased, that there was rejoicing in heaven, and that He was smiling down at us all.

A couple of weeks later, as we visited another underground church on the coast, we learned that some of the nonlocal Arab Christians attending our meetings would not be able to do so any longer as they were being persecuted for their faith at their jobs and where they lived. This was becoming unbearable for them, not only for them but also for all of us as a family. We tried to call them but it was in vain as they did not want anyone to know that they were still conversing with us.

In fact, up in the northern kingdom, we heard news about one of our Filipino brothers being caught by the police for propagating the good news of Jesus Christ. This created fear in every believer's heart in the Middle East, but at the same time it pumped our adrenaline to maximum acceleration. We just had to be patient and wise in every decision and action we took. We could only testify to God's faithfulness in each matter. He kept His promise—He never forsook us and neither did He leave us.

One of the questions that recurrently came up with our Muslim colleagues was, "If you are good, then why aren't you a Muslim?" The perception in the Middle East is that every Muslim is supposed to be good, and if someone isn't good, he or she is not a Muslim. So when they saw good people in other faiths, they were confused, and their query as to why they were not Muslims implied that non-Muslims are not really good people. You could not really blame them for such a mindset because they had been taught from childhood that non-Muslims are kafirs and infidels; therefore, they cannot be good people.

We needed God's wisdom to be able to answer this question wisely and yet not offend anyone in the process. I usually responded to my friends by saying, "You don't have to be good to know and be acceptable to God. You just have to have a longing heart for Him and He will make you good and new. If we were good without Him, then what is the use of having God in our lives? If He hasn't done any work in our lives, then what is the purpose of having Him in our lives? We can be gods too, can we?" I didn't come across anyone who didn't accept that answer; in fact, it set the ball rolling and made them think deeply about this fact and question their own faith.

All these years doing the Lord's work was not only exciting but also dangerous. The stakes were extremely high—we risked our lives to preach the good news of Jesus Christ every day. But it also gave us great joy, and the joy of the Lord was our strength and kept us energized for long periods of risky ministry. But God continually visited us in supernatural and profound ways.

CHAPTER 15

DIVINE ENCOUNTERS

The angel of the Lord encamps all around those who fear Him, and delivers them.

Psalm 34:7

For He shall give His angels charge over you, to keep you in all your ways.

Psalm 91:11

While returning home late one night through the dangerous mountainous terrain after ministering in the northeastern towns, and witnessing one of the most powerful meetings we have ever had, Maureena and I got a flat tire that brought the vehicle to a halt. Even though we were in an area that was well-known for deadly scorpions, poisonous snakes, and tribal groups that are hostile to outsiders and non-Muslims, the tire still had to be changed. But since I had a lot of experience changing tires throughout the years, I was able get it changed pretty quickly.

But then I also discovered another problem: we were stuck in the sand. The more I tried to drive the vehicle out, the deeper it dug into loose rock and dirt. With no way to extricate the vehicle, we sat in the cab and prayed. Shortly thereafter, headlights appeared in the review mirror, which was uncommon at this time of the night in this part of the country.

I sensed that I should not try to stop the approaching vehicle. As the vehicle drove by, we noticed it was full of young Arab men. The potential for trouble was great, and a sense of relief passed over us as they drove on into the night. As the taillights faded, I was prompted by the Holy Spirit to stop the next vehicle.

Within a matter of minutes, headlights again appeared in the rearview mirror and I stepped out in blind faith. With my hand, I cautioned the vehicle to stop. A man in a long, flowing, white dishdasha,[28] wearing a turban on his head, and a hooded, white windbreaker that obscured his demeanor, stepped out.

"We are stuck here and our vehicle isn't coming out," I said. "The more we try to run it, the deeper it sinks into the sand." There was no response from him at all—and I couldn't even see his face.

He got into the driver's seat of our vehicle and examined the positioning of the gears. I then handed him a towrope, which he took and then placed his vehicle in front of ours, connecting the two. We got into our vehicle and he got into his, then he slowly pulled forward and got us unstuck. Both the vehicles halted, and as soon as I removed the towrope, the stranger drove off even before I could thank him.

I tried my best to catch up with the man, but he kept getting further and further ahead. The congregants of the underground church would refer to me as "the king of the road," and I had never met anyone in my entire travels who could beat me on these roads. But that night I met someone who far surpassed me. And I remembered Jacob's wrestling match with the angel of the Lord who surpassed him in a showdown. Soon, the taillights of the man's vehicle disappeared and so did its tracks.

I was aware of all the routes around the area, even the secret ones in the jabels, and there was no place he could have turned off. We were totally shocked, yet praised God for answering our prayer in a timely manner by providing us with protection, care, and help. I still question whether or not he was an angel. This incident helped me reflect on how God had sent angels to deliver His people when they were in dire straits throughout history.

I also thought of the angel sent to free Sadhu Sundar Singh in the middle of the night when he was locked in a dark, dry well in Tibet. On the third day, however, he heard a voice from the top of the well, telling him to take hold of the rope that was being let down for his rescue. As the rope reached him, he grasped it with all his remaining strength, and was strongly but gently pulled up to the fresh air above. When he arrived at the top of the well, the lid was drawn over again and locked. As he looked around, his deliverer was nowhere to be seen; the clean air filled him with new life. All that the sadhu felt able to do was praise God for His wonderful deliverance.

We also thanked and praised God for His wonderful deliverance that night, for His mercies are new every morning and His faithfulness has surely endured.

We were then able to get off the dirt track and get onto the highway, very close to our hometown.[29]

After traveling for a few more minutes, we saw an army platoon pitched on the highway. As we drove closer, I slowed down as they motioned us to stop. I got out of the vehicle and they asked me, "Where are you coming from, and where are you going?"

"We are coming from the northwestern town after visiting our friends," I replied, "and are proceeding to our home in this vicinity."

They asked me to open all the doors of the vehicle so they could inspect our belongings; and when they saw Maureena sitting in the passenger's seat, they became cautiously respectful and did not hold us any longer. What a powerful meeting we had in the northwestern towns that night.

We were tested in the wilderness—even Satan tried his antics to thwart the godly things that took place that night, trying to discourage us. But upon reflection of the events of that night, we could only see spiritual warfare blatantly being played out and praised the Lord, for we won! When God is with us, then who can be against us?

Rashid, an Arab Muslim friend from school, with whom I had discussions about faith, was coaxing me to go and watch the movie The Passion of the Christ, as he was going to watch it with his friends soon. So I began to wonder why this movie was being screened in the Middle East. Apparently, it was released there only a couple of months after it was released in the rest of the world. Why so?

The default standard since ages has been that no Christian movie has been allowed to be screened in public, not even the "JESUS" movie, The Bible, or even The Ten Commandments. So why was the The Passion of the Christ getting luxury treatment? The anti-Semitic reviews from the West had enhanced the process of the public screening in the Middle East. What a wonderful public tool to evangelize the Muslim crowd in the Islamic countries! Maureena and I had been so engrossed with work and ministry that we had forgotten the rest of the world existed outside of what we were involved with.

One day, while school was in progress and we were all having our break time, Rashid requested everyone in the staff room to quiet down, as he was about to make a public statement. The silence drew him to talk. He said, "Yesterday, I went to the capital city with some of my friends to watch The Passion of the Christ. To see the prophet Issa's love, compassion, gracious heart, pain, and sufferings on the cross made me question my own life and faith. I desire to make a confession and proclamation. Will you guys allow me to do it?"

There was a consensus reply, "Sure, go ahead, Rashid; we are all ears."

What he said shocked me and blew me away. "Hereafter, I am going to follow Christ as my prophet, hero, and Savior," he said. "Does anybody have any problems with this?"

There was a deafening stillness as no one responded. Nobody, in their wildest dreams was expecting this so they didn't know how to react. I covered my face and hid it under the table, thinking folks in the room would suspect me of treason in converting Rashid. But no one even paid any attention to me—all eyes were on the confessor.

While he watched the movie, God did something in his heart that no one could do. He had proclaimed his own death. I didn't really know what would happen to him. People thought he was kidding at first, but he told us that he was serious and not backing out. Rashid's act triggered me to go and watch The Passion of the Christ with Maureena.

Within two weeks, and with a few days left for The Passion of the Christ to be taken off public screening, we were in the capital, ready to watch the movie. For years we hadn't watched a movie in a cinema—this was almost a brand new experience for us. As we waited patiently for the earlier show to get over, I observed some of the local secret Christians I knew turn up at the doors of the hall. I found out they were there every day for all of the shows.

The previous show got over, and awestruck people in tears were filing out. I even overheard some of them say, "Our prophet was so enduring and loving to have undergone such agony and persecution." I saw secret Christians sneak in and prayer walk the entire cinema hall before the next show began. We watched the movie through, enduring the agonizing plight of Christ portrayed on the screen. We could hear people sniffing and sobbing as the movie progressed.

Surely the prayers of the secret believers were working and doing wonders. It overwhelmed us that

Christ was being publicly exalted and glorified in a nation closed to Christianity. This also endorsed the fact that only God can do and get anything done when He desires to, even when the circumstances may not be conducive.

The night vigils in our town were picking up great momentum as people had started to come in swarms to attend these six- to seven-hour meetings that started late at night and wound down in the wee hours of the morning. Word of mouth was doing countless wonders for our advertising. We avoided keeping the footwears outside our home so that neighbors and people driving by would not get any ideas of what was going on inside. Without fail, God showed up at these meetings and the body of Christ was abundantly blessed.

During one such meeting, as we progressed in praise and worship, people cried and some even praised in languages they did not understand. People read randomly from Psalms and other biblical references, providing great spiritual food and words of encouragement to the hearers. As the meeting advanced late into the night, God started to reveal new things about the people in our living room.

God asked a lady to return to her home country, and another would be having her husband join her from overseas in just a short period. God put a prophetic word upon my tongue for a lady named Palak that night. I said, "You are pregnant and you don't even know about it because you are not expecting to have another child. This child conceived in you is a male child and this is the word of the Lord. You are to dedicate and bring this child up in the ways of the Lord so that when he grows up, he will not depart from His ways but serve the Lord God all the days of his life."

The next working day, Palak visited the gynecologist and found out that she was indeed pregnant. It was not yet time to know the sex of the child, and the couple didn't even intend to know—their faith in what God revealed was firm and strong. After we visited them, Palak's husband, Pashu, told me, "Brother, we will surely raise our son in the leading of the Lord and keep him dedicated and separated for serving Christ our Lord." This brought great joy to our souls.

When nine months were up, I was back in the hospital visiting Palak after she gave birth to another son. I gathered the naked child in my arms, raised him to heaven in dedication, and prayed for him and his parents—that God would give them the strength and wisdom to raise this child for the Lord. What immense joy it gave us to see the word of the Lord coming to fulfillment. Today, that couple lives in Ireland and are raising their children in the ways of God.

An outbreak of fresh fire was profoundly evident in the underground church. The intensity of the raging inferno was elevating every day and consumed anyone that came in its path. The enemy's camp was being intimidated and challenged as large numbers of Muslims, Hindus, Buddhists, Sikhs, Catholics, atheists, and nominal Christians were being saved in almost all the meetings leading up to mid-2004. God's abundant grace was always sufficient for us.

CHAPTER 16

CALLED TO BE MISSIONARIES

Go therefore and make disciples of all the nations, baptizing them in the name of the Father and of the Son and of the Holy Spirit, teaching them to observe all things that I have commanded you; and lo, I am with you always, even to the end of the age.

Matthew 28:19–20

Every soul with Christ is a missionary; every soul without Christ is a mission field.

—Unknown

With the support of our wives, Brother Ebenezer and I were planning a scouting trip to the southwestern region to gather information and to potentially extend the underground churches in that region. If we could gradually move into these areas, then we would also gain access to the oil fields and be able to minister to the people working there. We needed a breakthrough though, and the only weapon of our warfare was prayer and fasting, which we had accomplished for months before embarking upon this challenge.

Early one morning we drove through the jabels to the northwestern front, and then slowly traveled south, meeting potential people whom we had earlier targeted. Some negotiations went well, whereas others did not even take off. We ended our trip with a worship meeting at a remote vicinity in the southern jabels.

As the meeting started with a powerful time of worship, I witnessed a lady and Maureena fall flat on the ground, resting in the Spirit.[30] Maureena was skeptical about such things, even though this was happening to her at the moment. God was causing her to experience something divine that she had never experienced before. All her doubts regarding people enjoying the presence of God in such ways came crashing down. People were also speaking in tongues as the presence of God was being mightily manifested that day.

After having a meal with the residents, Brother Ebenezer and I prayed and reflected upon what had transpired throughout the day as we were returning home. God was telling us to wait longer; we would probably have to make a similar trip in the future to gauge and assess the situation further.

On December 31, 2003, our night meeting began exactly at 10 p.m. at a remote building on the periphery of our hometown. We immediately jumped into praising and worshiping our Creator. Just like every year during this night vigil, the underground body of Christ in the Middle East stayed on their faces for hours, interceding for many corporate and personal needs. One of the agendas was to ask God to sweep Europe and the United States with a spiritual awakening.

During one such occasion, all I could do was lift my hands in gratitude. I cannot quote any of the prayers that were prayed that day—most of the guttural cries I heard were indecipherable. Christians in the East are not only privy to the declining marriage, family, moral, and ethical ways of the West, but also of the Western church.

I remember Shanti's passionate prayer from the pews, when she asked God to send more people from the East to take the gospel to the nations that had evangelized them. Many Americans today (and many Europeans too) think they live in a progressive, intellectual, enlightened society—and that Christians in the developing world are the ones who are backward.

But it's beginning to appear that America and Europe are the real mission fields. I just hope and pray that more of us on the western side of the globe will join our Christian brothers and sisters, getting facedown on the floor. How God will work this out is the question. We are sure that nothing is too difficult for Him and neither was His hand shortened that He cannot save. He will move and do things in His own perfect time.

The room was overflowing with people as I delivered the New Year's message for 2004. I preached from Zechariah 4:6. As soon as the sermon was over, people had already started to praise God and respond to His Word. With tears flowing down their faces and humility in their hearts, many fell to the floor in devoted worship. There was a mighty move of the Holy Spirit as the gifts of the Spirit had started to flow. Prophetic words and the word of knowledge were being imparted to various souls. By 3 a.m. we all were quietly retreating to our homes.

On the first of January, 2004, my wife and I went into the Arabian jabels to pray, meditate on God's Word, and spend some time in praise and worship. Though we had our own personal time and space in the jabels, we came together after a while to share notes. God was telling us to go to the United States as missionaries to re-evangelize and revive the American church. Why was He sending us to the United States? Or why would He send any foreigner to America when 95 percent of the world's pastors live there?

We showed our reluctance to God by saying, "We are very happy here, though every day our life may be on the line. But this has become our comfort zone. We are not going to move till You move us. You have to do all the work and push us to be there, otherwise it might seem to the onlooker that we were self-imposing and proclaiming this call upon our lives and working toward it." I am sure God heard that prayer as we had challenged Him, showing our obstinacy to move out of our comfort zone.

Here is a quote from my journal that day:

> Maureena and I spent a wonderful time at the dam in the jabels. God was telling me that He was sending us as missionaries to the USA. This was something difficult to comprehend and believe, as once the US sent out missionaries to other parts of the world. It was now payback time for the good they had done in the past. God has not forgotten their investment in

the extension of His kingdom. Now they are in a crisis and dire need. The people their forefathers ministered to will now minister to them. They need to get back to God, which will then complete the circle as well as the assignment over them as a nation.

The choice to obey or not was still ours, however. The biblical passages that follow are the ones that God brought to my notice that day to encourage and strengthen us, and to testify to what He had disclosed to us:

> "Surely you shall call a nation you do not know, and nations who do not know you shall run to you, because of the Lord your God, and the Holy One of Israel; for He has glorified you." Seek the Lord while He may be found, call upon Him while He is near.
>
> Isaiah 55:5–6

> Fear not, for I am with you; be not dismayed, for I am your God. I will strengthen you, yes, I will help you, I will uphold you with My righteous right hand.
>
> Isaiah 41:10

> Surely He shall deliver you from the snare of the fowler and from the perilous pestilence.
>
> Psalm 91:3

> And the Lord said to Joshua, "This day I will begin to exalt you in the sight of all Israel, that they may know that, as I was with Moses, so I will be with you."
>
> Joshua 3:7

We sat for days without talking or moving toward what God had revealed to us. I received an e-mail from Gordon-Conwell Theological Seminary, telling me that they had a vacant spot for me to come on campus and do my studies. In fact, I had even forgotten that I had submitted my application there a couple of years ago, seeking their advice on the matter. We thought that since God was already moving us in that direction, we consented to be there. I received all the needed documents from the seminary to proceed to the American embassy in the Middle East.

During this whole time we didn't share this matter with anyone, save Brother Ebenezer and Ambu. We all continued in corporate prayer, seeking God's guidance and leading, especially for the person who would interview us at the embassy. In the middle of the week, Brother Ebenezer, Maureena, and I proceeded to the American embassy in the capital city for our interview.

Being a post-9/11 era, we were apprehensive on being given a visa for studies in the USA. As we entered the embassy, there were a number of security hoops that we encountered but finally arrived in the lobby. We came across numerous dejected and discouraged people who had been turned down for a visa to the States. This disheartened our spirits, but we intended to move ahead in the leading of the Holy Spirit.

After submitting our completed forms and documents, we moved to the waiting area and were summoned for an interview with the counselor after 20 minutes. During the interview, the counselor asked us a couple of personal, short, self-explanatory questions, which he happened to answer himself while browsing through our documents. He did not give us an opportunity to open our mouths and the interview was wrapped up within five minutes. We were asked to collect our student visas the next day.

What had just happened? I thought to myself. I had never attended any interview like that in my life. We could only see God's mighty hand in what He was accomplishing on our behalf. He was paving the way and setting the stage right there in our midst.

The next day we picked up our passports, which had a five-year visa stamped on them. We couldn't fathom what God was doing!

The first thing that followed was that my mentor made all the underground churches aware of our call to the United States, and that we would be leaving the Middle East by June of that same year. On hearing this news, most of the congregants were in pain, agony, and despair—their love and compassion overwhelmed us and brought us to tears. We had even forwarded our resignation to our workplaces three months prior to our leaving, and our colleagues and bosses were in awe and never imagined that we would be leaving after spending so many years in the Gulf.

We soon had a grand farewell party, and it helped us to see how the government really valued and appreciated our many years of service to their land and people. At the same time, the last association of our meetings in the Middle East had begun and people were bidding farewell to us. We could not comprehend the fact that God would use us as powerful instruments to weaken and destroy the enemy's stronghold before we moved.

Many of the people articulated that we didn't need to go to the United States as there was a dire need in the Middle East too. But God's plans could not be thwarted either.

I remember a testimony of a lady during our last few days in the Gulf, saying, "We thank God that He did not give you both children, otherwise you would have not taken the time or gone through the pain to travel these long distances to minister to us and our families. We fully appreciate all your time, energy, and investment that you poured into our lives."

One gentleman came up to me and said, "Brother, you are already doing more than most full-time pastors; you do not need to be theologically trained for what God is already doing through you both."

I responded by saying, "I know and understand your heart; but it is a matter of God's call and we are just responding to Him in obedience."

There were others who came up and told us not to go to the USA, as we would be giving up good jobs, going without any work, and putting all of our savings on the line without knowing what the outcome would be. The question we had was whether or not it would be worth the risk to take for the Lord. We could only respond by stepping out in the dark by faith, depending on Christ to assist us to walk on water.

Two months before we left for the States, I got a call from North India inviting me to be the director (CEO) of a Christian school/technical institute. The salary perks and facilities were amazing, and Maureena would not need to work. We would have everything that a person desires in a top-level job. We had to decide whether we were going to go to India with this lucrative offer or proceed to the United States with nothing.

We pictured ourselves going to both places. Obviously, both avenues were Christian but the risk was extremely high in going to America. We could see Satan's ploy in our return to India—he thought that he gave us an offer we could not refuse, an offer that looked "Christian" and very rewarding, but had no part to serve God in extending His kingdom.

After much prayer and seeking assistance from our mentors, we decided to move to the States. It was obvious that Satan was using his last card to disengage us from the call so that God's plan in our lives would be thwarted. With him no risks were involved, but with God the risk factor was really elevated.

If our flesh had taken over, we would surely be returning to India. It was important for us that we walk and move in the power of the Holy Spirit. We could see the parallels of Satan's offer to Jesus after He came back from fasting in the desert.

Matthew writes of that event:

> Again, the devil took Him up on an exceedingly high mountain, and showed Him all the

kingdoms of the world and their glory. And he said to Him, "All these things I will give You if You will fall down and worship me."

Then Jesus said to him, "Away with you, Satan! For it is written, 'You shall worship the Lord your God, and Him only you shall serve.'"

Matthew 4:8–10

The answer was very apparent to us! We had to follow and be obedient to God's call, not man's voice or lucrative offers. But what would lie ahead for us? There was so much still unknown.

CHAPTER 17

MAKING THE MOVE

So he answered and said to me: "This is the word of the Lord to Zerubbabel: 'Not by might nor by power, but by My Spirit,' says the Lord of hosts".

Zechariah 4:6

And how shall they preach unless they are sent? As it is written: "How beautiful are the feet of those who preach the gospel of peace, who bring glad tidings of good things!".

Romans 10:15

With the entire underground church being aware of our upcoming departure, almost every day somebody would be at our home bidding us their personal farewells by spending time in prayer, fellowship, ministering to one another, and shedding tears. The process was really heart-wrenching.

Gradually, however, we began to sell and give away many of our belongings. We were counting down the days until we would leave. The day finally arrived for our departure, and all the congregants of our town assembled at our home to see us off. We had a time of prayer and worship, and then drove to the airport with four suitcases. To our surprise, there were busloads of congregants from other parts of the Middle East that came to see us as well before we left. We all prayed in the lobby, then we checked in our luggage and proceeded to board the plane.

Maureena and I were not really talking to one another at this time, as we were so overwhelmed with how quick things were moving and the nostalgic memories of our life and ministry in the Gulf were rushing by. Mixed feelings soared as our time drew near to leave the Middle East. The people and the pristine land had stolen our hearts during those years. A part of us wanted to stay back, but a swift reminder of God's Word came into my mind, setting us back on track: "The spirit indeed is willing, but the flesh is weak" (Matthew 26:41).

The thought of separation from ministry, which was our baby and lifeline, was hitting us slowly by impacting our appetite, which had practically vanished. God had trained, shaped, and used us for 14 years to minister to His people in the Middle East, and now we were leaving after pioneering and establishing about ten underground churches in the Gulf region. By God's grace, we had also raised up and trained the second line of command to kick in when we left. God had accomplished what He desired from us in those years of ministry; and to come out from there undiscovered and unscathed was His miracle alone.

After flying throughout the night, our first stop was in Zurich, Switzerland. The stay over at the airport for a number of hours gave us the opportunity to look around and see the surroundings, which seemed to be so beautiful and refreshing after having resided in the dry, arid, hot wilderness of the Middle East for such a long time. After switching planes and crossing the Atlantic, we headed to Boston where we received our luggage before proceeding to Iowa to spend some time with my sister and her family, recuperating from our hectic schedule and travels.

We had two weeks of rest and then we were headed back to Boston. We received some bad news from the Middle East: one of the gentlemen I mentored was nabbed by his boss at his workplace for reading some Christian material online. His case was investigated and all the contacts on his cell phone were interrogated while he and his family were deported to their home country. If we were still in the Middle East, we would now be on the government's radar. But knowing what was to come, God had protected us from the trouble.

Knowing not a soul in Massachusetts and having no ministry whatsoever, we were like fish out of water. At times Maureena would weep but kept interceding for the USA, just like she had done since the 9/11 attacks.

One of the first things I did was locate Pastor Harrison in western Iowa, who had walked the same trail of ministry a couple of decades before we did. I apologized on behalf of the congregants living in the northwestern part of the Middle East region that had persecuted and shunned him when he traveled for hours to minister to them. Before that time, they had no one to give them spiritual food or quench their thirsty soul. The people in the Middle East recognized their mistake and showed remorse by desiring to set things right; therefore, they asked me to apologize on their behalf when I found him.

Studying for a masters in divinity at Gordon-Conwell required a lot of hard work. Formally learning biblical Greek was exhausting, and I had reached a turning point on whether or not to continue. Maureena's continual prodding and encouragement for me to stay focused gave me the courage to stay the course.

I also simultaneously started to work for a media service, which kept me busy around the clock. We began to attend Pilgrim Church, where God gave us an opportunity to minister to the youth, conduct an adult Sunday school class, and preach occasionally. Seeing the demand and prospects of Maureena to continue her nursing career, she started preparing for her nursing and English proficiency exams, and ended up passing with flying colors.

All of our funds were almost exhausted by July of 2005, and we would be on the streets if God did not act fast. We prayed and God faithfully answered our prayers in His time, not ours. After finding work in Beverly, Massachusetts, Maureena's job agents saw the potential for us to obtain a permanent resident status in the States. They got all our paperwork and formalities taken care of, and Maureena started to work in September of that year. In less than three months, we had our green card and were also getting theologically ready for ministry.

I stopped working for the media service by this time so that I could whole-heartedly concentrate on completing my studies as quickly as possible. Occasional joint and bone pains had made Maureena visit her doctor when, after some tests, they confirmed that she had rheumatoid arthritis and would have to be on medications for the rest of her life.

During early 2006, I enjoyed studying biblical Hebrew and was faring well when we learned through Maureena's radiology report that the doctors were suspicious of her contracting breast cancer. This nerve-wrenching experience brought my Hebrew grades to absolute lows, and I requested to retake the tests, which the professor gladly allowed me to do. All these things could have easily distracted and discouraged us from what God intended to do with our lives. But we knew God has called us here…and we knew He would continue to be faithful to us.

We continually spent time in prayer and worship, seeking God's leading in every matter of our lives. After Maureena got a biopsy and the results came back negative, we breathed a sigh of relief and thanked God for His amazing protection during a close call. My grades in biblical Hebrew just revealed how my life was entwined, attached, and impacted by the well-being of my wife.

Though the divinity program was four years long, I would be wrapping it up in under three years as I had been taking more courses than usual, studying through the summer and winter months, and making no time for entertainment. The only thing I seemed to do during those years was study, study, and more study.

God began to use us to do an internship and assist in pastoral duties at a Korean church in downtown Boston. In addition to all of this, people on campus began to ask where we would be going for ministry. We had absolutely no idea—but we knew God would pave the way in His time. We were just waiting for His marching orders.

During the summer of 2006, when Brother Ebenezer was visiting Pasadena, California, to wrap up his studies, we thought of visiting Los Angeles and Arizona to discern the prospects of ministry in that region. We traveled to LA and then visited Phoenix and Tucsan with our mentors. With our wives, Brother Ebenezer and I spent a lot of time praying whether God was calling us to that part of the world to minister to folks. We felt it was not to be and so returned to Boston, satisfied and encouraged from our brief visit to the West Coast.

As graduation was about to take place in six months, leaving the seminary campus was mandatory and we had started to check out the nearby accommodations. Though I had offers to return to the Middle East, to continue Ph.D. studies from the UK, and teach at a seminary in the US, I did not apply for any pastoral positions. I didn't consider it as a job but a calling; and one was not required to sign up as a hireling, but one that God would assign and show the way.

God already had a plan for us, and that plan became increasingly clear one November night. God kept me awake—sleep was not even on the radar. I got out of bed on that cold, snowy night, and was down on the floor silently praying and worshiping God. He told me that I was to go and shepherd Valley Church in Iowa, whose pastor was being called home that night. I was being convicted by the Holy Spirit to intercede for his soul as he was dying.

As I was not aware of everything that was going on the next morning as Maureena got up to go to work, I told her what had transpired that night and what God desired of us. Though she was reluctant to move from New England, we both agreed on just obeying God at every point of our life, no matter the sacrifices and costs we had to bear.

I called my sister in Iowa to inquire about the pastor of Valley Church, and she told me that everything was just fine. That morning I dozed off for a couple of hours, and got up just before noon to learn from my sister that the pastor of Valley Church was taken to a hospital the previous night with some illness that he had been suffering from. And he had passed away that morning. This left us all bewildered but in awe of God's wisdom and profound call upon our lives.

That Christmas season we were visiting my sister and her family in Iowa, and I was asked to bring the Christmas and New Year's messages for Valley Church. As we were returning from Iowa, the Valley leadership asked me when I was graduating from seminary. It would be in the summer of 2007, I told them. We were then summoned by Valley Church to candidate for the pastoral position so we would have to come for an interview and preach at their church, which we gladly did at the end of February.

During the interview, the interim pastor from Des Moines asked me, "How can you, being of Indian descent, pastor an American church that is predominantly white?"

My thoughts were racing as I was tempted to ask him how a white man could ever think of going overseas and evangelizing and pastoring a church in Africa or Asia? But I simply said, "For God there is no race or national hurdles; these are created by man. In the sight of God, no matter who we are, everyone is equal."

We returned to Boston and waited for the leadership to decide and announce their results. As I would be graduating by the end of that semester, the seminary director for pastoral position placement summoned me to her office where I made her aware to what was going on with our lives and the interview process. After some research, she warned me not to accept the offer at Valley Church. I probably did not give her a satisfying reply, but I said, "This is not my call but God's; so I have no control over it except to choose to obey or not."

She had no answer or advice to follow-up with, so I left her office. As the search committee of Valley Church could not reach a final verdict, they called us again for an interview in April. This time, the pastoral search team was brand new and composed of both trustees and deacons. Some of them were aware of the previous interview and apologized for the delay. They also apologized on behalf of the interim pastor who had asked the offensive question.

During this interview, one of the trustees asked me, "Why do you want to move to Iowa?"

I responded by saying, "I don't want to come here, but God never gives choices to His people. He just tells us what to do and this is what God has revealed to me." The interview did not last long, but they made me aware of the church funds and what was going on in the church, hoping that it would become easier for me to make the choice.

After some elderly congregants had dreams and visions of me being their new pastor, the trustees left a message on my phone while we were flying to Boston. It played back, "Congratulations! You are our new pastor." The next morning they called back and said, "We are sorry we forgot to ask you whether you would like to be our next pastor or not."

"God has given me no choice," I said, "and if I am not obedient to His call, just like Jonah, I will end up in the belly of the fish. It is always wise and in our favor when we obey His voice."

I had already started to pastor Valley Church remotely from Massachusetts. Though they desired us to there by May, I could only take on the pastoral role completely in June, after I had completed my graduation. My nephew Sunny came to pick us up from Boston and we took him on a short tour of New England before we made a two-day journey to Iowa.

The first Sunday of June 2007, I delivered the message from the pulpit of Valley Church. I could see the thirsty, hungry, and parched souls there who desperately needed a shepherd, and God was ready to provide.

We only knew that we were there in God's calling, and what He was about to do we could not even fathom. We could only meditate on His Word: "Eye has not seen, nor ear heard, nor have entered into the heart of man the things which God has prepared for those who love Him" (1 Corinthians 2:9). We were now living as missionaries in the Midwest. We had come so far.

CHAPTER 18

RESPONSE OF THE AMERICAN CHURCH

The harvest truly is great, but the laborers are few; therefore pray the Lord of the harvest to send out laborers into His harvest.

Luke 10:2

Any church that doesn't support missions will one day become a mission field.

—Anonymous Professor, GCTS, MA

Having served the underground church in the Middle East for 14 years and the American church in different capacities since 2004, I can very well see things not only as an outsider but as an insider too. Therefore, we will leave no stone unturned as we discuss the role and response of the American church to missions, not only overseas but domestically as well.

We must understand that we are looked up to by the global body of Christ as the one who leads them. So, naturally, how we respond as a leader in the mission of the church nationally and internationally will set the tone and standard for the rest of the world.

How we respond to the need of missions in the Middle East and in closed nations is not only critical for the underground churches, but for the actual survival of the American church as well. This is so it does not become a potential mission field itself. I want to give you a few reasons of how we can possibly respond to missions in closed and restricted regions.

The first is my interceding for missions and missionaries. Interceding in prayer is missionaries' number one need they have from a supporting church. Paul presses us to keep on "praying always with all prayer and supplication in the Spirit, being watchful to this end with all perseverance and supplication for all the saints" (Ephesians 6:18). One of the main jobs of the church is to ensure people are praying—both individually and corporately—for the missionaries that have been sent out.

The purpose is not to pray casual prayers like, "God, please be with our missionaries, help them, protect them, and meet their needs." These are important, but we must be praying in the Spirit for them as well (Romans 8:26). Our prayers should be passionately seeking their protection and welfare so that they are effective in their respective mission fields.

We may not realize it, but prayer backing is one of the most important necessities for any missionary—they could be in any adverse situation at any particular time, and therefore left at God's mercy to resolve their extrication. Our continual intercession for their lives can assist in their well-being.

During our ministerial trips within the Middle East, we came across a number of adverse situations that could not have been resolved without the persistent prayers of our intercessors. These intercessors are the backbone and strength of any ministry, and the best of them are never celebrated enough.

Being a casual intercessor is as good as being nothing at all. If God calls you to this effort, do not hesitate to jump in and be faithful, praying without ceasing for these souls whose lives hang by the string. We must not forget the encouragement intercessors get through their faithful service—your reward is not of this world but heavenly.

The second way we can respond to missions in closed countries is through funding missions. Jesus's ministry in the Middle East was very much scaling the highest peaks of the mountains.

Having lived for eight years when I was a teenager in the Himalayas, and having driven beyond the Rohtang Pass, which is more than 10,000 feet high, I know what it means to get into higher altitudes. The higher one climbs, the presence of oxygen reduces, which affects breathing, mobility, and the agility of any individual. Even carrying oxygen on one's back doesn't solve the problem. It becomes important for people to stay for a longer time in order to get immune to that environment.

When people climb peaks like Mount Everest, they usually camp out at the base for a couple of weeks in order to practice and train their bodies to endure the treacherous climb and back. I had a friend in the 1970s whose uncle made a fatal climb on Mount Everest, and that is what taught us the risks and fortitude it takes to accomplish an almost impossible mission.

Yet, unlike climbers being acclimatized on Mount Everest, the disciples were not waiting for some natural process to ready them for their assignment. They needed "power from heaven" and nothing less (Acts 1:8; Luke 24:49). Without God's own power, which is given through the Holy Spirit, no one can successfully do God's work on the earth.

In a sense, the wind of the Spirit is like the oxygen cylinders that enable climbers to reach the top of Mount Everest. And though a few can scale this peak without additional oxygen, we cannot succeed in our mission without the Spirit of God giving us power. But don't despair! If you have put your trust in Jesus as Lord and Savior, then you have already received the Holy Spirit. You have an unlimited supply of God's oxygen!

Unlike the first disciples in Jerusalem, you do not have to wait for anything to come down from heaven. We have been empowered. We have been sent. We are ready to go. But there needs to be people who will equip and supply the necessary tools needed for ministry in such perfidious mission fields.

Therefore, educating your local church body about the material needs of the missionaries you support is essential. Unfortunately, most churches are very passive in this area. Missionaries and potential missionaries often feel like they have been left out on a limb to fend for themselves, especially when even a little help from the pulpit would go such a long way. Encouraging people to become laborers for the harvest but not providing a means to get there is like evangelism without discipleship (Matthew 9:37).

In fact, during the end of the twentieth century, some of the underground churches that we ministered to in the Middle East were instrumental in buying back Christian slaves from Muslims in Sudan and adopting independent pastors and evangelists in developing countries to remunerate their salaries.

There are many churches that might be in a situation where it is not fiscally responsible to support a missionary or put them up for adoption to the body, which is fine. Adoption is not only about finances, but it is about relationship. If your church is in this situation, you might still offer to support a missionary through prayer and encouragement. Later, when your church is in a position to financially support them, then you already potentially know the character of a possible candidate to support.

I have often had churches refuse to talk to potential missionaries just because they can't support them financially. There are times where churches are supporting too many missionaries, but if this is not the case, adopt a missionary without any financial commitment anyway. When we fund and bless the missionaries, blessings begin to snowball—not only will you be a blessing for many, but the ones you support will become a blessing for others in their own community, creating a chain reaction of the blessing of God.

A third way we can respond to missions in closed countries is through self-transformational mission trips. Staying connected to missionaries can assist in arranging short-term trips for people from your church to have a glimpse and taste of what ministry is like in another country. This can also get people interested in staying for a longer spell or becoming completely devoted to missions.

However, it is sad to see many churches in the West that have made these short-term trips sound and look more or less like some charity, recreational, or entertainment tours. Short-term trips are a time where we go serve other people in the various cultures they find themselves in.

I continually come across people who go to the mission field with the intent of being a blessing to those people, but in the process get blessed before returning to their home country. A couple of years ago a teenage friend of our nephew went to Tanzania for a short-term mission trip during his summer vacation. After arriving in Tanzania, he lost his route to the destination but somehow found his way around. He stayed and survived for two months without really having the basic necessities of life. He said, "It was a hard life, but the endurance made me a man, and a man who is now yearning for God. It taught me to have faith in God."

It is quite evident that dire circumstances and insufficiency draws us to complete dependence on God. He went on to say, "What I could not have learned in a lifetime in America, I learned within two months in Africa. I thought I would help out and be a blessing to these guys in Tanzania, but the reality is that they were a great blessing to me." After talking to him more,

I realized that he had returned as a completely transformed man.

And there are many similar stories of people returning from short-term mission trips. Because of these testimonies, I don't like to call these trips short-term mission trips, but rather self-transformational mission trips.

These self-transformational trips can potentially ignite a desire and discern a call for people to devote their lives for longer periods in closed mission fields. We must not forget that only about 50 percent of all long-term missionaries complete their first term of commitment and keep going. Consequently, communication and encouragement are vital to long-term success.

Staff and church members responsible for missionary care are to be the encouragement point needed to monitor communication between the missionary and the body. They need to ensure that the missionary is receiving the care they need. It could be something as simple as ensuring e-mail communication and updates are occurring, or making sure a place is prepared for the missionaries when they return from the field, causing them to feel welcomed.

People who spend longer time in the mission field usually feel a sense of detachment from their extended families and even from their home countries. For them, being a citizen of their birth country or any other country doesn't really matter, as they know they are just passing through this world and are citizens of heaven.

Their attachments are more to their spiritual families out in the mission field with whom they seem to have a profound connection. The church needs to recognize and facilitate these attachments in their lives. This is their lifeline and keeps them not only entwined with people but with the God they serve.

These people will serve God faithfully through any circumstance, and also prepare the next generation whom they intend to pass the baton to. The church should make it a point to honor and recognize their sacrificial service to people they didn't know and had no idea would become an integral part of their lives. Though they may be humble to recognize it, this will encourage and keep them passionately serving God.

After 25 years as a missionary in Africa, Samuel Morrison was coming home on the same ocean liner that brought Teddy Roosevelt back from an African hunting expedition. The dock, where the great ship pulled into the New York Harbor, was jammed with what looked like the entire population of New York City. Bands were playing, banners were waving, choirs of children were singing, multicolored balloons were floating, and newsreel cameras were poised to record the return of the president.

Mr. Roosevelt stepped down the gangplank to thunderous cheers, applause, and a shower of confetti and ticker tape. If ropes and police had not restrained the crowd, he would have been mobbed!

But at the same time, Samuel Morrison quietly walked off the boat. No one was there to greet him; he simply slipped through the crowd alone and unnoticed. Because of the crush of people there to welcome the president, Morrison couldn't even find a cab. So he began to complain in his heart: "Lord, the president has been in Africa killing animals for three weeks and the whole world turns out to welcome him home. I've given 25 years of my life to Africa, serving You, and no one has greeted me or even knows that I'm here."

In the quietness of his heart, Samuel heard a gentle, loving voice that whispered, "But My dear child, you're not home yet!"[31]

One of the biggest blessings a church can do for a missionary is give them the opportunity to report what God has been doing in and through their ministry. Give your missionaries some time in a service so they can share all that has been taking place. It helps them feel like the work they are doing for the Lord is noticed, appreciated, and important. It also lets the church body know about the investment they have made. At the end of Paul's missionary journey, it was a common practice for him to report to the entire church all that the Lord had done (Acts 14:27; 15:41 21:19).

The church should also occasionally invite missionaries to share from God's Word and what God has laid upon their hearts for the congregants. These missionaries not only bring exciting stories, but a perspective of God that we may have never encountered or seen in our lives, which will encourage people seeking to embark on short- or long-term mission trips. Their passion and experience of the mission field can trigger hearts to become passionate for God and potentially serve Him with an undaunted zeal. Those who seem to be laid back and sleeping in your congregations may just wake up from a long slumber and become serious for God.

The zeal of these missionaries can easily rub off on your congregation. Therefore, I encourage the churches to invest in the missionaries' lives so that in time they will invest in your church. I have witnessed many churches trying to avoid giving opportunities to missionaries to share God's Word on a Sunday morning. But be assured, it will never hurt to give them opportunities to speak to your congregation.

Finally, one of the ways churches can connect with missions is to prepare and send people from their church to the mission field they support. They will be a source of encouragement for the missionaries, and also a follow-up on behalf of the church.

On arriving at their destination, they might be overwhelmed as they start experiencing things they have never experienced before. They will get a first-hand visual of the work these missionaries do. How we respond to the missionaries and their work will impact them a great deal. So we must be sensitive to how the missionaries operate in that part of the world.

Impulsively giving our own opinions to the missionaries may be inappropriate at this point, as they have been in the mission field for a long time and know the pros and cons of their specific operations. What these partners can do, however, is experience things on their own and then share their experience when they come back. They can put forth their questions before these missionaries who will be more than willing to share their experiences and make them aware of things which they might never learn till they have been there for a longer period of time.

Remember, these partners are there not only to serve while being there, but they are to return back to their home church with information and experiences they will share with the supporting congregation members. On hearing their testimonies, the members of the congregation will probably be boosted to invest more in missions through their money and time. At the same time, they will be crediting the church for the good work they have been doing by investing in missions to the unreached through these missionaries.

With the voice of the Western church almost stunted and the wavering impact of the pulpit in the public eye, we can easily foresee the gradual decay and demise of the influence of the church in society. The silence of many pastors and ministers in America on issues that are vital to God and every human heart, including their neglect of missions, is paving the way for the American church to be paralleled with the church of Europe.

With many Western churches becoming more of a platform for entertainment and fun, many Christians in our country have already testified to the fact that no matter how mega or micro our church may seem, we are quickly becoming a potential mission field. God recognizes this fact and is importing foreign missionaries to America from nations and continents that were once impacted by Western missionaries.

These missionaries are reconciled to the fact that it is their payback time. God knows that America was founded on Judea-Christian teachings and is faithful in bringing external uninhibited fearless voices crying out in the spiritually dry and parched land to restitute and restore that which is lost, thus completing the entire circle of events.

How the American church responds to these voices is crucial, as it will set the stage and determine the fate of the Western church in future generations. This could be God's last call to save the body of Christ in America from decaying. We desperately need to redefine the vision of the global church.

CHAPTER 19

GLOBAL CHURCH VISION REDEFINED

Where there is no vision, the people perish: but he that keepeth the law, happy is he.

Proverbs 29:18 KJV

But seek first the kingdom of God and His righteousness, and all these things shall be added to you.

Matthew 6:33

We can do any amount of studies to try and define what the predicament in the Middle East really is, but as long as we cease from confronting it as a spiritual problem, the results are going to be fruitless. When we comprehend and recognize it as a spiritual quandary, however, we can then tackle it on a different dimension altogether.

Sending troops for war to try to curb the Middle East conflict will only settle the problem temporarily. When this happens, the problem is only dealt with on the surface, but the core of it is still breeding snake eggs. Settling the score in the physical realm doesn't achieve permanent results; it only negates who we really are. If we act and behave in the same manner as our enemy, then how are we any different from them? We are just playing their game of tit for tat.

In order to make progress, we have to look at it from a spiritual perspective, keeping in mind the bigger picture of the long-term negative consequences that our actions will breed. The next generation will only encounter and reap that which they didn't initiate or sow. Being worldly unwise but seeking divine wisdom, I suggest that the American church being inclusive of the global church and the "Christian" nations can pursue and tackle the Middle East problem with the strategy I present in this chapter and the next.

Just as former President George W. Bush took the war to the soil of the enemy, we also have to sneak into their trenches and win them for Christ. Having resided in those trenches for a long time, Maureena and I understand what it takes to accomplish a successful underground mission.

During our ministry tours and interactions with people in the core of the Middle East, we came across a number of secret missionaries and tentmakers from several Asian and African countries. But we rarely ever met anyone from the West. This supports the factual findings that though the West is the leader in sending out Christian missionaries and tentmakers, it has now been matched by missionaries from South Korea and "non-Christian" countries like China and India.

Even churches in African countries have woken up and excelled in targeting their missions to the churches in Europe. This resounds a wake-up call to the sleeping giant—the American church—and calls for speedy action. This awakening could save the Western church from becoming fossilized.

We will redefine the global church vision, its mission, implementation, and implications. The church is welcome to adopt and implement this vision in a system that is conducive to their particular circumstances.

Our redefined vision is to win the Middle East and closed nations for Christ. Our main objectives and goals are to raise, mentor, train, equip, empower, and commission a new generation of missionaries and tentmakers in order to evangelize and win the hearts of the people in the Middle East and closed nations to the gospel of Jesus Christ.

The countries in the West have always been lured by black gold to maintain a formal and diplomatic high profile presence in the Middle East. Not forgetting that Christ commissioned the church to reach out to the ends of the world, the global church can commission many more people to the Middle East and accomplish different tasks effectively without the formal garb of diplomacy, thus saving all the unnecessary formalities to accomplish their mission. Though people from the West may be on their radar, they won't be under suspicion as long as they are not associated with the government.

But why should we focus on and target the Middle East? There are a number of reasons for this, though I will only give a few of them below. The first reason is that we can restore the land. Let me explain what I mean.

God created the Garden of Eden and placed Adam and Eve in the heart of the Middle East. Our forefathers and prophets of the Old Testament walked throughout the land; the fragment of the Wailing Wall and the Temple Mount rests in the land. Christ was born and ministered in the Middle East before His ascension, and the New Testament apostles and churches were planted right there before the Islamic takeover.

As my wife and I visited and interacted with the bedous[32] living in the mountainous regions of the Gulf, we learned that their forefathers were possibly Jews or Christians and had been driven into the mountains by the Islamic perpetrators because of their noncompliance to their faith. But as years went by, Sharia law was enforced and they yielded to the Islamic faith with resistance. In order to live in the land, it became mandatory for any permanent resident to be a Muslim. Because of this, it becomes not only a matter of concern but also urgency on the part of the global body of the Christ to surreptitiously insinuate the Middle East and reclaim those lost souls for Christ.

The second reason we should focus on the Middle East is because of the presence of Israel there. After 1,900 years of dispersion, persecution, and oppression, the Jewish people finally achieved statehood. They did it in spite of the incredible economic and political challenges that faced the new nation and the military opposition by overwhelming numbers of their neighbors' intent on Israel's destruction. Even today, the threat of the neighboring Islamic nations doesn't go unnoticed, especially the continual attacks of Hezbollah and the intimidation of annihilation from the Iranians.

When Israel was proclaimed a nation in 1948, a hundred biblical prophecies sprang into life. I will just give one as an example:

> Then say to them, "Thus says the Lord God: 'Surely I will take the children of Israel from among the nations, wherever they have gone, and will gather them from every side and bring them into their own land; and I will make them one nation in the land, on the mountains of Israel; and one king shall be king over them all; they shall no longer be two nations, nor shall they ever be divided into two kingdoms again.'"
>
> Ezekiel 37:21–22

This Scripture has been fulfilled in the twentieth century. Israel has a state and a nation but no king. And they will not have a king until the One whom God has promised rises up. Since the statement follows immediately concerning the formation of the state of Israel, the event in 1948 is the precursor to the second advent of Jesus Christ.

Zechariah prophesies about Israel coming to Christ in the last days as well:

> And I will pour on the house of David and on the inhabitants of Jerusalem the Spirit of grace and supplication; then they will look on Me whom they pierced. Yes, they will mourn for

Him as one mourns for his only son, and grieve for Him as one grieves for a firstborn.

Zechariah 12:10

Winning the Jews for Christ should be one of our major objectives and a short-term goal for the global church. How the body of Christ pursues this when Israel is constantly under fire is of utmost importance. This agenda should never ever be removed from the mission of any global church.

The third reason we should focus on the Middle East during this time is because of the return of Christ is dependent upon it. Luke is clear about the physical nature of Christ's ascension in the book of Acts—and he says that Jesus would return in the same manner as He departed. So it was insisted that He would physically return.

Luke writes:

> Now when He had spoken these things, while they watched, He was taken up, and a cloud received Him out of their sight. And while they looked steadfastly toward heaven as He went up, behold, two men stood by them in white apparel, who also said, "Men of Galilee, why do you stand gazing up into heaven? This same Jesus, who was taken up from you into heaven, will so come in like manner as you saw Him go into heaven."

Acts 1:9–11

To this affect the Old Testament prophet Zechariah had already prophesied Christ's second coming:

And in that day His feet will stand on the Mount of Olives, which faces Jerusalem on the east. And the Mount of Olives shall be split in two, from east to west, making a very large valley; half of the mountain shall move toward the north and half of it toward the south.

Zechariah 14:4

The global church needs to trust God by shifting from sending mission trips to places where the risks and financial investment is minimal to where the need is greater and more faith is required. From biblical documentation and prophecy, we are aware that Christ will ascend and prevail in the physical realm during His second coming at the Mount of Olives, which stands opposite to Jerusalem in the east.

Being aware of the contemporary events that lead to the last days and that set the stage for the second coming of Christ, it becomes more apparent as demands prompt action on the part of the global church to reassess their missional pursuits, reorganizing and spearheading evangelistic missions in the Middle East.

We are also called to adhere to the Great Commission: after Jesus's resurrection, He ascended from the Mount of Olives shrouded by a cloud, and sat at the right hand of the Father. But before He left, He commissioned His disciples, saying:

All authority has been given to Me in heaven and on earth. Go therefore and make disciples of all the nations, baptizing them in the name of the Father and of the Son and of the Holy

Spirit, teaching them to observe all things that
I have commanded you; and lo, I am with you
always, even to the end of the age.

Matthew 28:18–20

And before that, Jesus said that "this gospel of the
kingdom will be preached in all the world as a witness to
all the nations, and then the end will come" (Matthew
24:14). This evidently elevates our passion and zeal for
diligently reaching out to the Jews, Muslims, and other
non-Christians around the world.

The reason why the global church needs to begin
focusing on the Middle East is simply because this is
the most unreached region in the world. The more we
sit on it and wait for someone else to come and do the
job, the more we become partakers in delaying the second coming of Christ. We have a lot of work to do and
so little time to do it in.

But are we up for this challenge? If we are, then we
have a lot on our plate to deal with. This arrays the platform for us to pursue a redefined global church vision.
But let us now turn our attention to how we pursue this
redefined vision.

CHAPTER 20

PURSUING THE REDEFINED VISION

Then the Lord answered me and said: "Write the vision and make it plain on tablets, that he may run who reads it".

Habakkuk 2:2

Brethren, my heart's desire and prayer to God… is that they may be saved.

Romans 10:1

It is my desire to now talk about how we can pursue the redefined vision of the global church by winning souls for Christ throughout the earth. Proverbs 11:30 articulates the truth that "the fruit of the righteous is a tree of life, and he who wins souls is wise." But we ask, "Why is it wise to win souls, especially the ones in America today?" It is because soul winning helps the believer in their walk with the Lord. It imparts the heart of God to them, and helps invigorate their faith.

It also helps the growth the body of Christ, because a church that is passionate about soul winning is a growing church. I remember one of my ministerial associates told me that a vibrant church is the sign of a live church—it will never die.

Winning souls also helps the community at large. When even a handful of Christians in a church get truly revived, the whole community benefits from the blessing. The contemporary condition of our communities reflects the status quo of the local body of Christ. In order for the community to flourish, the body of Christ in that region has to flourish as well.

Another reason winning souls is wise is because it helps the overall health of the nation. The writing is on the wall and it goes without saying that we have dug a pit for ourselves. The present climate of our country reflects the dire condition of the pulpit and pastors in America. The awakening and renewal needs to begin here before it spills out into the marketplace.

And finally, soul winning accomplishes the final instructional commission of Jesus Christ to all His followers. As the prophet Isaiah says, "Go through, go through the gates! Prepare the way for the people; build up, build up the highway! Take out the stones, lift up a banner for the peoples!" (Isaiah 62:10). With all the necessary resources available in our nation, this will further prepare, equip, and pave the way for many more souls to be won in other nations around the world.

The second way we pursue the redefined vision of the church is to make fishers of men. The one who finds Christ and then follows Him must inevitably become a fisher of men. "And Jesus said unto them, Come ye after me, and I will make you to become fishers of men" (Mark 1:17 KJV).

Jesus apparently made His rowdy, incompetent, and illiterate disciples gospel preachers in order to save souls. Studying Christ's tutelage methodology, we too will be able to lead many souls to our Savior if we follow His example. Here Jesus advanced a fundamental theory of making fishers of men, and we must understand it if we are to become competent and effective evangelists. Christ's model serves the needs for all evangelists globally.

His method laid the foundation to allow His disciples to set the best example for us. We all know that actions speak louder than words. Therefore, Jesus motivated His disciples to put all His teachings into practice so that they would do as He did to them, making them fishers of men. When Jesus walked the earth proclaiming the good news, He called His disciples first and made them fishers of men before they went out spreading the good news of the gospel.

Jesus practiced a disciplined lifestyle, taught and exemplified with prayer, fasting, faith, teaching, and operating in the gifts of the Holy Spirit. This profoundly rubbed off on the disciples who did the same thing while preparing and raising the next generation.

The global church must exemplify Christ through their lives while preparing men and women to be effective evangelists. This will assist the church to evangelistically become a corporate soul winner domestically and overseas, impacting communities and the nations for Christ. As these fishers of men win souls for Christ, there is always joy and a banquet in heaven.

According to Matthew 28:18–20, we reconcile the fact that each and every Christian is assigned with the commission to win souls. And one of the questions Brother Ebenezer used to ask me at the end of every year was this: "Ajai, how many souls for Christ this year?" He went on to affirm that this is the question that Christ will ask us when we meet Him face to face. This should not only warn us, but also encourage and motivate us to become and make fishers of men.

We also pursue the redefined vision of the church by raising up strong men and women for God. We live in an era where we see that we have almost lost two generations in a row. Are we raising a generation where men don't know how to be gentlemen and women don't know how to be ladies?

The stereotypical male and female under 30 years of age is one who is clutching a beer bottle, chasing one another, and being sex freaks that cannot differentiate between that which is sane and insane. Discipline, learning, and work ethics seem to be distant from them; they don't even understand these terminologies. Therefore, it makes it more urgent for contemporary parents to raise strong men and women for God who will be completely given over to their Creator.

It is important today's parents stop being selfishly focused on themselves and understand the dire situation we face as a nation of completely losing this generation to the world—the divorce rate and broken families attributing highly to this cause. We have to focus on our offspring so that we can raise them up in the ways of the Lord. We are reminded in Proverbs: "Train up a child in the way he should go, and when he is old he will not depart from it" (Proverbs 22:6). We can understand why the contemporary generation is what it is—we just didn't do our part.

It is a great sacrifice and challenge to raise a new generation for Christ and in His teachings. Exemplifying Christlike ways, patience, and longsuffering toward them will heap coals of fire upon their heads and surely win them for Christ. This action will not only encourage but motivate them to be drawn to Christ. The responsibility of raising a strong generation falls upon all our shoulders so that we can joyfully pass the baton to a responsible group of people who will faithfully and diligently carry out the work of the Lord after we are gone.

The fourth way we pursue the redefined vision of the church is by discipling individuals. God chooses men and women who will give up the rights to their own lives and be willing instruments to be used for His purposes. The sad side of this is the fact that many leaders today in the church have isolated themselves and have not trained anyone to take their place.

If we are concerned about God and His work, we will take painful steps to raise up and usher in people who are passionate about God. Training them in the likeness of God is the inclination, not what the world is looking for in them. On-the-job training is important and essential to be effective in what we do.

Learning from people who have gone before them is imperative, as this will build them up with strong foundations under their feet. Not only will they acquire their own experiences but be richly embedded with the experience of their predecessors. They will not only learn from their own mistakes but from the ones who went before them, thus making them wiser than ever before. This rich heritage will further enhance the speedy growth of God's kingdom.

"Tentmaking" refers to the activities of any Christian who, while dedicating him or herself to the ministry of the gospel, receives little or no pay for church work, but performs secular jobs to support themselves by working full time in the marketplace with their skills and education. It is vital for every person on the team to be trained professionally in some way or the other. This will assist in their daily subsistence and endurance in the mission field.

They will not have to beg or depend upon the church or its supporters for financial aid. Though it is painstaking and burns the candle at both ends, being professionally trained in another field keeps one independent from all strings that might become a hindrance in furthering the ministry.

The common professions in demand in the Middle East are medical, nursing, education, marketing, sales, and management. One can opt for getting professionally trained in a subject of their interest and gifted field so that they can land a job and work with ease while at the same time doing the Lord's work. My wife was a trained and licensed nurse, whereas I was trained as a teacher. Both of these jobs helped us survive and do the work of the Lord independently. People who have walked this road before and have researched and worked in the Middle East will have the ability to guide the strengths of these men and women in the right direction.

Without being professionally trained in any related field, it is next to impossible to work in the Middle East as an underground tentmaker. These volunteers must be thoroughly trained and experienced to do secular jobs and spiritually fit to extend God's kingdom in an underground ministry setting.

It is important that we assist in discerning an individual's call. The Word of God clearly teaches that God calls the weak to confound the wise (1 Corinthians 1:26–31); so if you have a calling on your life, it is because God chooses people that are incapable of producing life qualities on their own that will be acceptable in His sight. It is possible for Him to do it through us when we give Him preeminence in our life.

Discerning someone's call is not related to their likes and dislikes, but whether God is really calling them for a particular purpose. I did not have the slightest inclination to ministry, not to mention underground ministry in hostile circumstances. Early in life, I knew God had a call upon my life but was rebelliously running away from it. I believed that it was the work of the pastors and evangelists to proclaim God's Word, and I had no business to be intrusive. But God brought us to the Middle East to learn the hard way, and our whole life was turned around with a whole new perspective on ministry.

Though I served the underground church for a number of years, it was my mentor, Brother Ebenezer, who helped me undergo the process of discerning the call. He chose some elderly and mature people in the faith to also help. The process lasted for a couple of years before it was finally determined. It was hard, but it was needed so that the church would avoid any ungodly and human intervention in the matter. We praised the Lord for His faithfulness and helping the underground church discern and raise another servant for God.

After commissioning and deployment, it is helpful to provide the missionaries with all the resources and support to help them achieve their objectives. For targeting specific regions in the Middle East and in closed nations, the leadership must lay hands upon them and pray for them, commissioning the team to move to their mission trenches while making sure that all resources and help are available to them to effectively achieve the mission objectives.

The church body at this time should be given up to prayer and fasting for the protection of these volunteers, that God would continually guard and minister to them as they go out to a ministry field that can be both dangerous and exciting.

While working as tentmakers, they can communicate important information to others on the team as well as begin or join an underground cell group. It is usually safe if they do not communicate ministerial matters with people in their home country. This can make the authorities suspicious of their presence in their country and potentially jeopardize the purpose they are there for. They can, however, communicate all matters to their leadership in their home country while visiting family during their annual holiday.

Joining an underground home group or starting one where there isn't any is a good place to start. Becoming an integral part of that group and impacting people at work with their behavior and work ethics can gradually open up windows for spiritual conversations.

Trust is a major factor on which the whole wheel of ministry revolves. Along the way they must discern who are going to be faithful to this call of ministry and thus make use of such people to extend God's kingdom. It is also imperative that they know whom they can talk to and what the limit is to which they can go. They must build a strong social rapport with the local community, especially with their colleagues, which will potentially further open doors to other people through them.

There is always a possibility of the footprint of ministry gradually enlarging and extending to a point of burning them out. Because of this, it is important for these men and women to be equipped to train the next generation so that they can take on some of the load of ministry from these overworking men and women.

After serving in the field for seven to ten years, it is important they return to their home country and train the next generation to facilitate the same objectives, thus continuing the cycle. These experienced men and women may return home after their services are terminated or resignation. If they have served in a field for a longer period of time to acquire the necessary experience and skill to effectively succeed in a mission, they should be put on the training team of the church to impart their experience and skills to the next team of volunteers.

This will not only engage, prepare, facilitate, and equip the next team, but also help them see the perspective of the people in the trenches before them. Thus the cycle of learning, mission accomplishment, and teaching will continue to the next generation. The invaluable training they will carry into the field will be a great asset and will also determine the success or failure of the mission before them.

If our focus is not on Christ and our vision is not extending His kingdom, then everything we do will be a failure. Keeping in mind that "where there is no vision, the people perish: but he that keepeth the law, happy is he" (Proverbs 29:18 KJV), we must keep marching forward. It is important for the body of Christ to understand that many lives are at stake and will perish eternally, consecutively delaying the coming of Christ if we do not reach out speedily to the ends of the earth for Christ our Lord, Savior, and King.

Working in the field as tentmakers burns the candle at both ends, tiring people out pretty quickly. Therefore, it is imperative for the body of Christ in the West to recognize this dilemma, and organize and implement restful breaks to these faithful men and women of God who put their lives on the line for Christ daily.

As we continually serve and raise up the next generation to serve as missionaries in the closed regions of the Middle East, we will witness a great move of God sweeping through that region. God is faithful, who will also do everything that He has promised and desired for that region.

EPILOGUE

"For My thoughts are not your thoughts, nor are your ways My ways," says the Lord. "For as the heavens are higher than the earth, so are My ways higher than your ways, and My thoughts than your thoughts".

Isaiah 55:8–9

"For I know the thoughts that I think toward you," says the Lord, "thoughts of peace and not of evil, to give you a future and a hope".

Jeremiah 29:11

The underground ministry was at its peak in 2003. A frenzy of revivals broke out in every nook and corner of the Persian Gulf. The venues of these meetings could no longer accommodate the throngs of people pouring in to be blessed and to be a blessing to others.

Brother Ebenezer and I had been given up to prayer. We devised a plan to expand the mission by taking on the whole nation. This meant reaching out to the neglected southern areas and the oil fields. We had a clear vision: the Gulf for Christ. Our goal was profound, but we rested in knowing that with God all things are possible.

Maureena and my minds were set and focused on our mission, yet God told us to leave the Middle East and move to the United States as missionaries. This came as a complete surprise to us; but reluctantly, we moved to the States in the summer of 2004. In the fall of the same year, Brother Ebenezer left to go to another nation in the Middle East.

We didn't really know why God was doing this until the 2005 cyclone hit. It destroyed parts of the Gulf Coast and completely altered the landscape of the region, which helped make things a little clearer for us. The physical devastation also changed the fate of the underground churches.

In addition, internal betrayal and an immoral socio-political climate brewed in the area. God had to deal with it before allowing His kingdom to extend in that nation. As we reflected on these events, we saw the parallels between our departure from the Middle East and Lot and his family leaving Sodom and Gomorrah at God's insistence.

In the previous years, we had witnessed numerous dictatorships being overthrown by the citizens of Islamic nations, which revealed how susceptible and fragile the leadership was from within. If the global church can comprehend and assimilate this fact, it can capitalize on the vulnerability of the Middle East. If the church can stimulate men and women within the body of Christ, commissioning them to take on the endeavor of a love-based covert outreach, it can potentially win the hearts of the people in the Middle East for Christ. Before we knew it, things could easily turn around for good. If we could captivate one Middle Eastern nation for Christ, the rest of them would follow suit.

If we comprehend and recognize the war in the Middle East as a spiritual predicament, we can tackle it on a different dimension altogether. Sending in the military isn't going to curb or resolve the problem. In fact, military efforts will arouse more hatred and vindictiveness for the West.

The body of Christ in the West needs to understand and apply Ephesians 6:12–13:

> For we do not wrestle against flesh and blood, but against principalities, against powers, against the rulers of the darkness of this age, against spiritual hosts of wickedness in the heavenly places. Therefore take up the whole armor of God, that you may be able to withstand in the evil day, and having done all, to stand.

The battle in the Middle East belongs to our Lord, but we need to learn to navigate it beyond the physical realm—at a spiritual level.

Maureena and I often wonder why God brought us to the States and not somewhere else. Why didn't He keep us in the Middle East? Studying the American spiritual condition helps us understand why He allowed this to happen.

America was built on Judeo-Christian guidelines. Our forefathers were dedicated to their Creator, but in the past few decades we have observed a gradual decline of the authority and impact of the church in America, thus paving the way for it to become a potential mission field. God saw our endearing passion and vision for the kingdom in the Middle East and turned it around for the nation that He loves so dearly and has His eyes upon.

God is setting the stage for a revival in the West. With 95 percent of the world's pastors living in America and the spiritual climate stunted, it is quite obvious why God is resorting to gradually bringing missionaries from progressive countries and strategically embedding them in different parts of the United States. Before an outbreak of revival can happen, it is mandatory it be preceded with the persecution of Christians, which is already in the making.[33]

God is already doing miraculous things in the Middle East today. There are many Muslims and non-Christians coming to Christ without evangelistic intervention or the use of the Bible, but through dreams and visions. Many people give testimonies of God awaking them in the middle of the night in order to talk to them, or meeting them in person while on the road to Mecca and Medina. There is an unprecedented desire and hunger amongst these people to seek after God and know the truth (Jesus Christ)—the truth that will set them free.

God is showing up in desperate situations and doing amazingly incomprehensible things that we have only heard of happening in pagan nations, but have never experienced ourselves.

If God has called America to lead other nations, then it must set its priorities straight. First, the country must be desperate for Him. It must leave its comfort zone and get down on its knees in submission and surrender to the King of all kings. Genuine passion to seek God will surely result in finding Him. The Western church needs to stop playing church and get serious with Him before everything goes haywire.

Let us not forget 1 Peter 4:17: "For the time has come for judgment to begin at the house of God; and if it begins with us first, what will be the end of those who do not obey the gospel of God?" Therefore, the body of Christ needs to humble itself. Leadership within the church needs to call for national prayer, fasting, and repentance so that God will forgive us, heal our land, and restore us. If we do not heed the voice of our Creator, then we are surely setting the stage for our nation to become a massive mission field.

If we lose focus and become complacent to pursue Christ's final commission as stated in Matthew 28:18–20, God will not become handicapped to accomplish His mission. He has the ability to make the rocks cry out. He can even revive the dead to complete that which is left undone.

Today, with the stories that we are hearing and the way events are unfolding in the Middle East, there is a great likelihood of a fiery revival waiting in the wings, which would give way to mass conversions and possibly turn the tables in the West. Therefore, Lord, we pray:

> Revive us again;
> Fill each heart with Thy love;
> May each soul be rekindled
> With fire from above.[34]

WE CARE ABOUT YOU!

Every time I preach I usually give an altar call or evoke the listeners to think about their lives and allow the Spirit of God to convict them to follow Christ by encouraging them to begin an intimate walk with Him. At times people respond positively, and many times there is no apparent response at all. But what is important is that God's Word has gone forth without returning void, and it will accomplish what He desires.

The most important question for ages has been whether we have surrendered our lives to Jesus Christ and made Him our King of all kings, Lord of all lords, and Savior. If we have believed in our hearts and articulated with our mouths that Jesus Christ is Lord, we are saved and born again. The next step is to grow in His Word, develop a lifestyle of prayer, and love Him with all our heart, soul, mind, and strength.

I would encourage you to intercede earnestly and support missions to closed and restricted countries, even for those who live in our own country, so that those potentially lost souls will be won for Christ. For each soul that is saved, there is a great celebration in heaven. And you are the one who facilitated it.

We would love to hear from you! To contact us, please write to:

Ajai and Maureena Prakash
P.O. Box 552
North Liberty, IA 52317
USA
Or you can reach us online at
ajaiprakash.tateauthor.com and www.thewellia.com.

GLOSSARY

azaan—call/rush to prayer

bedous—Bedouins

burkha—an enveloping outer garment worn by women in some Islamic traditions to cover their bodies when in public

dhaba—roadside restaurant

dishdahsa—a long usually white robe traditionally worn by men in the Middle East

jabel—mountain

Ingeel—Arabic word for The Bible

Issa Masih—Jesus Christ

kafir—unbeliever

madrassa—an Islamic school

Masihi—Christian

mullah—Islamic cleric/clergy/priest/rabbi

sadhu - holy man

sari—a strip of unstitched cloth worn by women, ranging from four to nine yards in length, that is draped over the body in various styles which is native to the Indian subcontinent

sharia—Islamic law

shura—consultation

sunna—the moral example set by the prophet Muhammad as recorded in the hadiths

sura—verse/text from the Qur'an

takfir—excommunication of other Muslims as infidels

ustad—teacher

wadi—valley/stream

ENDNOTES

1   This was in Ludhiana, Punjab, India.

2   Mussoorie is about 180 miles west of Ludhiana, which was where our home was located.

3   This studio happened to be the annex of a house in Sarabha Nagar, which is in the most posh area of Ludhiana.

4   This is the norm for many people living in developing countries during this time.

5   This clipping was so small it was actually hard to even read the print on the paper.

6   This is a little roadside restaurant.

7   William L. Cleveland, *A History of the Modern Middle East* (Colorado: Westview Press, 2004), 464.

8   My grandfather, who had been living with my parents since my grandmother went to be with the Lord, loved us very much. He could not reconcile the fact that Maureena would be leaving soon for the Middle East in the midst of all the turmoil.

The shock was so profoundly unbearable that he had a stroke and was bedridden for the rest of his life.

9   At that time, India did not have cable or satellite television; therefore, we did not have any international channels but wholly depended upon the local network of two to three available government run television stations. It was all black and white television. Apparently, the Western world was watching all of the war live on cable network and also in color. The war had also earned the nickname "Video Game War" after the daily broadcast images onboard the American bombers during Operation Desert Storm.

10   He was an engineer pursuing to be a potential pastor.

11   Ambu was an ESL teacher for the government.

12   He now presently resides in Switzerland.

13   This camp took place at Sewait, Allahabad, India.

14   A *madrassas* is an Islamic school.

15   This endorsed the word in Jeremiah 33:3: *"Call to Me, and I will answer you, and show you great and mighty things, which you do not know."*

16   This reminded me of John the Baptist's words about Christ: *"He must increase, but I must decrease"*

(John 3:30). My greatest desire was to live out these words.

17 A burkha is an enveloping outer garment worn by women in some Islamic traditions to cover their bodies when in public. The face-veil portion is usually a rectangular piece of semi-transparent cloth whose top side is sewn to corresponding portion of the head-scarf, so that the veil hangs down loose from the scarf. This can be turned up if the woman wishes to reveal her face (otherwise the whole face would be covered). In other cases, the *niqab* can be a side-attached cloth that covers the face below the region of the eyes.

18 In reality, we actually held these on another day of the week, not Sunday itself.

19 The first Eid of the year is known as Eid Al-Fitr. It marks the end of the month of Ramadan, which is the month Muslims fast every day from sunrise to sunset. The holidays usually last seven to nine days, beginning immediately after Ramadan is over.

20 Please refer to 1 Kings 9:28, 10:11, and Job 22:24 for references to this area.

21 It looked like they were looking right through us.

22 *Jabels* are mountains.

23 Passages like Isaiah 9:8–21 support the above understanding and are strewn throughout God's Word.

24 This was a call to prayer.

25 This is the Arabic word for a Bible.

26 The length of days depends upon the sight of the moon.

27 To win a Muslim for Christ during Ramadan could be equated to one of the most heinous crimes someone might commit in the United States—like premeditated murder. There is a gravity to proselytizing someone for Christ in the Middle East, especially during the month of Ramadan.

28 A long, white robe traditionally worn by men in the Middle East.

29 Reflecting upon that pitch-dark night still sends shivers down my spine. It also gives me sheer joy for being visited and assisted by an angel.

30 Some people identify this as being "slain in the Spirit."

31 Anne Graham Lotz, *Heaven: My Father's House* (Nashville, TN: W. Publishing Group [Division of Thomas Nelson], 2001), 14–15.

32 Bedouins.

33 This has been observed in biblical narratives and also a global observation for revival outbreaks in other countries.

34 John Jenkins Husband and William Paton MacKay, "Revive us Again." Public Domain.